Administrative Law: A Very Short Introduction

VERY SHORT INTRODUCTIONS are for anyone wanting a stimulating and accessible way into a new subject. They are written by experts, and have been translated into more than 45 different languages.

The series began in 1995, and now covers a wide variety of topics in every discipline. The VSI library currently contains over 750 volumes—a Very Short Introduction to everything from Psychology and Philosophy of Science to American History and Relativity—and continues to grow in every subject area.

Very Short Introductions available now:

ABOLITIONISM Richard S. Newman
THE ABRAHAMIC RELIGIONS
　Charles L. Cohen
ACCOUNTING Christopher Nobes
ADDICTION Keith Humphreys
ADMINISTRATIVE LAW
　Stephen Thomson
ADOLESCENCE Peter K. Smith
THEODOR W. ADORNO
　Andrew Bowie
ADVERTISING Winston Fletcher
AERIAL WARFARE Frank Ledwidge
AESTHETICS Bence Nanay
AFRICAN AMERICAN HISTORY
　Jonathan Scott Holloway
AFRICAN AMERICAN RELIGION
　Eddie S. Glaude Jr.
AFRICAN HISTORY John Parker and
　Richard Rathbone
AFRICAN POLITICS Ian Taylor
AFRICAN RELIGIONS
　Jacob K. Olupona
AGATHA CHRISTIE Gill Plain
AGEING Nancy A. Pachana
AGNOSTICISM Robin Le Poidevin
AGRICULTURE Paul Brassley and
　Richard Soffe
ALEXANDER THE GREAT
　Hugh Bowden
ALGEBRA Peter M. Higgins
AMERICAN BUSINESS HISTORY
　Walter A. Friedman
AMERICAN CULTURAL HISTORY
　Eric Avila
AMERICAN FOREIGN RELATIONS
　Andrew Preston
AMERICAN HISTORY Paul S. Boyer
AMERICAN IMMIGRATION
　David A. Gerber
AMERICAN INTELLECTUAL
　HISTORY
　Jennifer Ratner-Rosenhagen
THE AMERICAN JUDICIAL SYSTEM
　Charles L. Zelden
AMERICAN LEGAL HISTORY
　G. Edward White
AMERICAN MILITARY HISTORY
　Joseph T. Glatthaar
AMERICAN NAVAL HISTORY
　Craig L. Symonds
AMERICAN POETRY David Caplan
AMERICAN POLITICAL HISTORY
　Donald Critchlow
AMERICAN POLITICAL PARTIES
　AND ELECTIONS L. Sandy Maisel
AMERICAN POLITICS
　Richard M. Valelly
THE AMERICAN PRESIDENCY
　Charles O. Jones
THE AMERICAN REVOLUTION
　Robert J. Allison
AMERICAN SLAVERY
　Heather Andrea Williams
THE AMERICAN SOUTH
　Charles Reagan Wilson
THE AMERICAN WEST Stephen Aron
AMERICAN WOMEN'S HISTORY
　Susan Ware

AMPHIBIANS T. S. Kemp
ANAESTHESIA Aidan O'Donnell
ANALYTIC PHILOSOPHY
    Michael Beaney
ANARCHISM Alex Prichard
ANCIENT ASSYRIA Karen Radner
ANCIENT EGYPT Ian Shaw
ANCIENT EGYPTIAN ART AND
    ARCHITECTURE Christina Riggs
ANCIENT GREECE Paul Cartledge
ANCIENT GREEK AND
    ROMAN SCIENCE Liba Taub
THE ANCIENT NEAR EAST
    Amanda H. Podany
ANCIENT PHILOSOPHY Julia Annas
ANCIENT WARFARE
    Harry Sidebottom
ANGELS David Albert Jones
ANGLICANISM Mark Chapman
THE ANGLO-SAXON AGE John Blair
ANIMAL BEHAVIOUR
    Tristram D. Wyatt
THE ANIMAL KINGDOM
    Peter Holland
ANIMAL RIGHTS David DeGrazia
ANSELM Thomas Williams
THE ANTARCTIC Klaus Dodds
ANTHROPOCENE Erle C. Ellis
ANTISEMITISM Steven Beller
ANXIETY Daniel Freeman and
    Jason Freeman
THE APOCRYPHAL GOSPELS
    Paul Foster
APPLIED MATHEMATICS Alain Goriely
THOMAS AQUINAS Fergus Kerr
ARBITRATION Thomas Schultz and
    Thomas Grant
ARCHAEOLOGY Paul Bahn
ARCHITECTURE Andrew Ballantyne
THE ARCTIC Klaus Dodds and
    Jamie Woodward
HANNAH ARENDT Dana Villa
ARISTOCRACY William Doyle
ARISTOTLE Jonathan Barnes
ART HISTORY Dana Arnold
ART THEORY Cynthia Freeland
ARTIFICIAL INTELLIGENCE
    Margaret A. Boden
ASIAN AMERICAN HISTORY
    Madeline Y. Hsu

ASTROBIOLOGY David C. Catling
ASTROPHYSICS James Binney
ATHEISM Julian Baggini
THE ATMOSPHERE Paul I. Palmer
AUGUSTINE Henry Chadwick
JANE AUSTEN Tom Keymer
AUSTRALIA Kenneth Morgan
AUTHORITARIANISM James Loxton
AUTISM Uta Frith
AUTOBIOGRAPHY Laura Marcus
THE AVANT GARDE David Cottington
THE AZTECS David Carrasco
BABYLONIA Trevor Bryce
BACTERIA Sebastian G. E. Amyes
BANKING John Goddard and
    John O. S. Wilson
BARTHES Jonathan Culler
THE BEATS David Sterritt
BEAUTY Roger Scruton
LUDWIG VAN BEETHOVEN
    Mark Evan Bonds
BEHAVIOURAL ECONOMICS
    Michelle Baddeley
BESTSELLERS John Sutherland
THE BIBLE John Riches
BIBLICAL ARCHAEOLOGY
    Eric H. Cline
BIG DATA Dawn E. Holmes
BIOCHEMISTRY Mark Lorch
BIODIVERSITY CONSERVATION
    David Macdonald
BIOGEOGRAPHY Mark V. Lomolino
BIOGRAPHY Hermione Lee
BIOMETRICS Michael Fairhurst
ELIZABETH BISHOP
    Jonathan F. S. Post
BLACK HOLES Katherine Blundell
BLASPHEMY Yvonne Sherwood
BLOOD Chris Cooper
THE BLUES Elijah Wald
THE BODY Chris Shilling
THE BOHEMIANS David Weir
NIELS BOHR J. L. Heilbron
THE BOOK OF COMMON PRAYER
    Brian Cummings
THE BOOK OF MORMON
    Terryl Givens
BORDERS Alexander C. Diener and
    Joshua Hagen
JORGE LUIS BORGES Ilan Stavans

THE BRAIN Michael O'Shea
BRANDING Robert Jones
THE BRICS Andrew F. Cooper
BRITISH ARCHITECTURE
    Dana Arnold
BRITISH CINEMA Charles Barr
THE BRITISH CONSTITUTION
    Martin Loughlin
THE BRITISH EMPIRE Ashley Jackson
BRITISH POLITICS Tony Wright
BUDDHA Michael Carrithers
BUDDHISM Damien Keown
BUDDHIST ETHICS Damien Keown
BYZANTIUM Peter Sarris
CALVINISM Jon Balserak
ALBERT CAMUS Oliver Gloag
CANADA Donald Wright
CANCER Nicholas James
CAPITALISM James Fulcher
CATHOLICISM Gerald O'Collins
THE CATHOLIC REFORMATION
    James E. Kelly
CAUSATION Stephen Mumford and
    Rani Lill Anjum
THE CELL Terence Allen and
    Graham Cowling
THE CELTS Barry Cunliffe
CHAOS Leonard Smith
GEOFFREY CHAUCER David Wallace
CHEMISTRY Peter Atkins
CHILD PSYCHOLOGY Usha Goswami
CHILDREN'S LITERATURE
    Kimberley Reynolds
CHINESE LITERATURE Sabina Knight
CHOICE THEORY Michael Allingham
CHRISTIAN ART Beth Williamson
CHRISTIAN ETHICS D. Stephen Long
CHRISTIANITY Linda Woodhead
CICERO Yelena Baraz
CIRCADIAN RHYTHMS
    Russell Foster and Leon Kreitzman
CITIZENSHIP Richard Bellamy
CITY PLANNING Carl Abbott
CIVIL ENGINEERING David Muir Wood
THE CIVIL RIGHTS MOVEMENT
    Thomas C. Holt
CIVIL WARS Monica Duffy Toft
CLASSICAL LITERATURE William Allan
CLASSICAL MYTHOLOGY
    Helen Morales
CLASSICS Mary Beard and
    John Henderson
CLAUSEWITZ Michael Howard
CLIMATE Mark Maslin
CLIMATE CHANGE Mark Maslin
CLINICAL PSYCHOLOGY
    Susan Llewelyn and
    Katie Aafjes-van Doorn
COGNITIVE BEHAVIOURAL
    THERAPY Freda McManus
COGNITIVE NEUROSCIENCE
    Richard Passingham
THE COLD WAR Robert J. McMahon
COLONIAL AMERICA Alan Taylor
COLONIAL LATIN AMERICAN
    LITERATURE Rolena Adorno
COMBINATORICS Robin Wilson
COMEDY Matthew Bevis
COMMUNISM Leslie Holmes
COMPARATIVE LAW Sabrina Ragone
    and Guido Smorto
COMPARATIVE LITERATURE
    Ben Hutchinson
COMPETITION AND ANTITRUST
    LAW Ariel Ezrachi
COMPLEXITY John H. Holland
THE COMPUTER Darrel Ince
COMPUTER SCIENCE
    Subrata Dasgupta
CONCENTRATION CAMPS
    Dan Stone
CONDENSED MATTER PHYSICS
    Ross H. McKenzie
CONFUCIANISM Daniel K. Gardner
THE CONQUISTADORS
    Matthew Restall and
    Felipe Fernández-Armesto
CONSCIENCE Paul Strohm
CONSCIOUSNESS Susan Blackmore
CONTEMPORARY ART
    Julian Stallabrass
CONTEMPORARY FICTION
    Robert Eaglestone
CONTINENTAL PHILOSOPHY
    Simon Critchley
COPERNICUS Owen Gingerich
CORAL REEFS Charles Sheppard
CORPORATE SOCIAL
    RESPONSIBILITY Jeremy Moon
CORRUPTION Leslie Holmes

COSMOLOGY Peter Coles
COUNTRY MUSIC Richard Carlin
CREATIVITY Vlad Glăveanu
CRIME FICTION Richard Bradford
CRIMINAL JUSTICE Julian V. Roberts
CRIMINOLOGY Tim Newburn
CRITICAL THEORY
  Stephen Eric Bronner
THE CRUSADES Christopher Tyerman
CRYPTOGRAPHY Sean Murphy and
  Rachel Player
CRYSTALLOGRAPHY A. M. Glazer
THE CULTURAL REVOLUTION
  Richard Curt Kraus
DADA AND SURREALISM
  David Hopkins
DANTE Peter Hainsworth and
  David Robey
DARWIN Jonathan Howard
THE DEAD SEA SCROLLS
  Timothy H. Lim
DECADENCE David Weir
DECOLONIZATION Dane Kennedy
DEMENTIA Kathleen Taylor
DEMOCRACY Naomi Zack
DEMOGRAPHY Sarah Harper
DEPRESSION Jan Scott and
  Mary Jane Tacchi
DERRIDA Simon Glendinning
DESCARTES Tom Sorell
DESERTS Nick Middleton
DESIGN John Heskett
DEVELOPMENT Ian Goldin
DEVELOPMENTAL BIOLOGY
  Lewis Wolpert
THE DEVIL Darren Oldridge
DIASPORA Kevin Kenny
CHARLES DICKENS Jenny Hartley
DICTIONARIES Lynda Mugglestone
DINOSAURS David Norman
DIPLOMATIC HISTORY
  Joseph M. Siracusa
DOCUMENTARY FILM
  Patricia Aufderheide
DOSTOEVSKY Deborah Martinsen
DREAMING J. Allan Hobson
DRUGS Les Iversen
DRUIDS Barry Cunliffe
DYNASTY Jeroen Duindam
DYSLEXIA Margaret J. Snowling

EARLY MUSIC Thomas Forrest Kelly
THE EARTH Martin Redfern
EARTH SYSTEM SCIENCE Tim Lenton
ECOLOGY Jaboury Ghazoul
ECONOMICS Partha Dasgupta
EDUCATION Gary Thomas
EGYPTIAN MYTH Geraldine Pinch
EIGHTEENTH-CENTURY BRITAIN
  Paul Langford
ELECTIONS L. Sandy Maisel and
  Jennifer A. Yoder
THE ELEMENTS Philip Ball
GEORGE ELIOT Juliette Atkinson
EMOTION Dylan Evans
EMPIRE Stephen Howe
EMPLOYMENT LAW David Cabrelli
ENERGY SYSTEMS Nick Jenkins
ENGELS Terrell Carver
ENGINEERING David Blockley
THE ENGLISH LANGUAGE
  Simon Horobin
ENGLISH LITERATURE
  Jonathan Bate
THE ENLIGHTENMENT
  John Robertson
ENTREPRENEURSHIP Paul Westhead
  and Mike Wright
ENTROPY James Binney
ENVIRONMENTAL ECONOMICS
  Stephen Smith
ENVIRONMENTAL ETHICS
  Robin Attfield
ENVIRONMENTAL JUSTICE
  Pamela Hill
ENVIRONMENTAL LAW
  Elizabeth Fisher
ENVIRONMENTAL POLITICS
  Andrew Dobson
ENZYMES Paul Engel
THE EPIC Anthony Welch
EPICUREANISM Catherine Wilson
EPIDEMIOLOGY Rodolfo Saracci
ETHICS Simon Blackburn
ETHNOMUSICOLOGY Timothy Rice
THE ETRUSCANS Christopher Smith
EUGENICS Philippa Levine
THE EUROPEAN UNION
  Simon Usherwood and John Pinder
EUROPEAN UNION LAW
  Anthony Arnull

EVANGELICALISM
  John G. Stackhouse Jr.
EVIL Luke Russell
EVOLUTION Brian and
  Deborah Charlesworth
EXISTENTIALISM Thomas Flynn
EXPLORATION Stewart A. Weaver
EXTINCTION Paul B. Wignall
THE EYE Michael Land
FAIRY TALE Marina Warner
FAITH Roger Trigg
FAMILY LAW Jonathan Herring
MICHAEL FARADAY
  Frank A. J. L. James
FASCISM Kevin Passmore
FASHION Rebecca Arnold
FEDERALISM Mark J. Rozell and
  Clyde Wilcox
FEMINISM Margaret Walters
FEMINIST PHILOSOPHY
  Katharine Jenkins
FILM Michael Wood
FILM MUSIC Kathryn Kalinak
FILM NOIR James Naremore
FIRE Andrew C. Scott
THE FIRST WORLD WAR
  Michael Howard
FLUID MECHANICS Eric Lauga
FOLK MUSIC Mark Slobin
FOOD John Krebs
FORENSIC PSYCHOLOGY
  David Canter
FORENSIC SCIENCE Jim Fraser
FORESTS Jaboury Ghazoul
FOSSILS Keith Thomson
FOUCAULT Gary Gutting
THE FOUNDING FATHERS
  R. B. Bernstein
FRACTALS Kenneth Falconer
FREE SPEECH Nigel Warburton
FREE WILL Thomas Pink
FREEMASONRY Andreas Önnerfors
FRENCH CINEMA Dudley Andrew
FRENCH LITERATURE John D. Lyons
FRENCH PHILOSOPHY
  Stephen Gaukroger and Knox Peden
THE FRENCH REVOLUTION
  William Doyle
FREUD Anthony Storr
FUNDAMENTALISM Malise Ruthven
FUNGI Nicholas P. Money
THE FUTURE Jennifer M. Gidley
FUTURISM Ara H. Merjian
GALAXIES John Gribbin
GALILEO Stillman Drake
GAME THEORY Ken Binmore
GANDHI Bhikhu Parekh
GARDEN HISTORY Gordon Campbell
GENDER HISTORY Antoinette Burton
GENES Jonathan Slack
GENIUS Andrew Robinson
GENOMICS John Archibald
GEOGRAPHY John Matthews and
  David Herbert
GEOLOGY Jan Zalasiewicz
GEOMETRY Maciej Dunajski
GEOPHYSICAL AND
  CLIMATE HAZARDS Bill McGuire
GEOPHYSICS William Lowrie
GEOPOLITICS Klaus Dodds
GERMAN LITERATURE Nicholas Boyle
GERMAN PHILOSOPHY
  Andrew Bowie
THE GHETTO Bryan Cheyette
GLACIATION David J. A. Evans
GLOBAL ECONOMIC HISTORY
  Robert C. Allen
GLOBAL ISLAM Nile Green
GLOBALIZATION Manfred B. Steger
GOD John Bowker
GÖDEL'S THEOREM A. W. Moore
GOETHE Ritchie Robertson
THE GOTHIC Nick Groom
GOVERNANCE Mark Bevir
GRAVITY Timothy Clifton
THE GREAT DEPRESSION AND
  THE NEW DEAL Eric Rauchway
THE GULAG Alan Barenberg
HABEAS CORPUS Amanda L. Tyler
HABERMAS James Gordon Finlayson
THE HABSBURG EMPIRE Martyn Rady
HAPPINESS Daniel M. Haybron
THE HARLEM RENAISSANCE
  Cheryl A. Wall
THE HEBREW BIBLE AS LITERATURE
  Tod Linafelt
HEGEL Peter Singer
HEIDEGGER Michael Inwood
THE HELLENISTIC AGE
  Peter Thonemann

HEREDITY John Waller
HERMENEUTICS Jens Zimmermann
HERODOTUS Jennifer T. Roberts
HIEROGLYPHS Penelope Wilson
HINDUISM Kim Knott
HISTORY John H. Arnold
THE HISTORY OF ASTRONOMY
　Michael Hoskin
THE HISTORY OF CHEMISTRY
　William H. Brock
THE HISTORY OF CHILDHOOD
　James Marten
THE HISTORY OF CINEMA
　Geoffrey Nowel-Smith
THE HISTORY OF COMPUTING
　Doron Swade
THE HISTORY OF EMOTIONS
　Thomas Dixon
THE HISTORY OF LIFE
　Michael Benton
THE HISTORY OF MATHEMATICS
　Jacqueline Stedall
THE HISTORY OF MEDICINE
　William Bynum
THE HISTORY OF PHYSICS
　J. L. Heilbron
THE HISTORY OF POLITICAL
　THOUGHT Richard Whatmore
THE HISTORY OF TIME
　Leofranc Holford-Strevens
HIV AND AIDS Alan Whiteside
HOBBES Richard Tuck
HOLLYWOOD Peter Decherney
THE HOLY ROMAN EMPIRE
　Joachim Whaley
HOME Michael Allen Fox
HOMER Barbara Graziosi
HORACE Llewelyn Morgan
HORMONES Martin Luck
HORROR Darryl Jones
HUMAN ANATOMY
　Leslie Klenerman
HUMAN EVOLUTION Bernard Wood
HUMAN GEOGRAPHY Patricia Daley
　and Ian Klinke
HUMAN PHYSIOLOGY
　Jamie A. Davies
HUMAN RESOURCE
　MANAGEMENT Adrian Wilkinson
HUMAN RIGHTS Andrew Clapham
HUMANISM Stephen Law
HUME James A. Harris
HUMOUR Noël Carroll
IBN SĪNĀ (AVICENNA)
　Peter Adamson
THE ICE AGE Jamie Woodward
IDENTITY Florian Coulmas
IDEOLOGY Michael Freeden
IMAGINATION
　Jennifer Gosetti-Ferencei
THE IMMUNE SYSTEM
　Paul Klenerman
INDIAN CINEMA Ashish Rajadhyaksha
INDIAN PHILOSOPHY Sue Hamilton
THE INDUSTRIAL REVOLUTION
　Robert C. Allen
INFECTIOUS DISEASE Marta L. Wayne
　and Benjamin M. Bolker
INFINITY Ian Stewart
INFORMATION Luciano Floridi
INNOVATION Mark Dodgson and
　David Gann
INTELLECTUAL PROPERTY
　Siva Vaidhyanathan
INTELLIGENCE Ian J. Deary
INTERNATIONAL LAW
　Vaughan Lowe
INTERNATIONAL MIGRATION
　Khalid Koser
INTERNATIONAL RELATIONS
　Christian Reus-Smit
INTERNATIONAL SECURITY
　Christopher S. Browning
INSECTS Simon Leather
INVASIVE SPECIES Julie Lockwood and
　Dustin Welbourne
IRAN Ali M. Ansari
THE IRAQ WARS Samuel Helfont
ISLAM Malise Ruthven
ISLAMIC HISTORY Adam Silverstein
ISLAMIC LAW Mashood A. Baderin
ISOTOPES Rob Ellam
ITALIAN LITERATURE
　Peter Hainsworth and David Robey
HENRY JAMES Susan L. Mizruchi
JAPANESE LITERATURE Alan Tansman
JESUS Richard Bauckham
JEWISH HISTORY David N. Myers
JEWISH LITERATURE Ilan Stavans
JOURNALISM Ian Hargreaves

JAMES JOYCE Colin MacCabe
JUDAISM Norman Solomon
JUNG Anthony Stevens
THE JURY Renée Lettow Lerner
KABBALAH Joseph Dan
KAFKA Ritchie Robertson
KANT Roger Scruton
KEYNES Robert Skidelsky
KIERKEGAARD Patrick Gardiner
KNOWLEDGE Jennifer Nagel
THE KORAN Michael Cook
KOREA Michael J. Seth
LAKES Warwick F. Vincent
LANDSCAPE ARCHITECTURE
    Ian H. Thompson
LANDSCAPES AND
    GEOMORPHOLOGY
    Andrew Goudie and Heather Viles
LANGUAGES Stephen R. Anderson
LATE ANTIQUITY Gillian Clark
LAW Raymond Wacks
THE LAWS OF THERMODYNAMICS
    Peter Atkins
LEADERSHIP Keith Grint
LEARNING Mark Haselgrove
LEIBNIZ Maria Rosa Antognazza
C. S. LEWIS James Como
LIBERALISM Michael Freeden
LIGHT Ian Walmsley
LINCOLN Allen C. Guelzo
LINGUISTICS Peter Matthews
LITERARY THEORY Jonathan Culler
LOCKE John Dunn
LOGIC Graham Priest
LOVE Ronald de Sousa
MARTIN LUTHER Scott H. Hendrix
MACHIAVELLI Quentin Skinner
MADNESS Andrew Scull
MAGIC Owen Davies
MAGNA CARTA Nicholas Vincent
MAGNETISM Stephen Blundell
MOSES MAIMONIDES Ross Brann
MALTHUS Donald Winch
MAMMALS T. S. Kemp
MANAGEMENT John Hendry
NELSON MANDELA Elleke Boehmer
MAO Delia Davin
MARINE BIOLOGY Philip V. Mladenov
MARKETING Kenneth Le
    Meunier-FitzHugh
THE MARQUIS DE SADE John Phillips
MARTYRDOM Jolyon Mitchell
MARX Peter Singer
MATERIALS Christopher Hall
MATHEMATICAL ANALYSIS
    Richard Earl
MATHEMATICAL BIOLOGY
    Philip K. Maini
MATHEMATICAL FINANCE
    Mark H. A. Davis
MATHEMATICS Timothy Gowers
MATTER Geoff Cottrell
THE MAYA Matthew Restall and
    Amara Solari
MEANING Emma Borg and
    Sarah A. Fisher
THE MEANING OF LIFE
    Terry Eagleton
MEASUREMENT David Hand
MEDICAL ETHICS Michael Dunn and
    Tony Hope
MEDICAL LAW Charles Foster
MEDIEVAL BRITAIN John Gillingham
    and Ralph A. Griffiths
MEDIEVAL LITERATURE
    Elaine Treharne
MEDIEVAL PHILOSOPHY
    John Marenbon
HERMAN MELVILLE Maurice S. Lee
MEMORY Jonathan K. Foster
METAPHYSICS Stephen Mumford
METHODISM William J. Abraham
THE MEXICAN REVOLUTION
    Alan Knight
MICROBIOLOGY Nicholas P. Money
MICROBIOMES Angela E. Douglas
MICROECONOMICS Avinash Dixit
MICROSCOPY Terence Allen
THE MIDDLE AGES Miri Rubin
MILITARY JUSTICE Eugene R. Fidell
MILITARY STRATEGY
    Antulio J. Echevarria II
JOHN STUART MILL Gregory Claeys
MINERALS David Vaughan
MIRACLES Yujin Nagasawa
MODERN ARCHITECTURE
    Adam Sharr
MODERN ART David Cottington
MODERN BRAZIL Anthony W. Pereira
MODERN CHINA Rana Mitter

MODERN DRAMA
    Kirsten E. Shepherd-Barr
MODERN FRANCE
    Vanessa R. Schwartz
MODERN INDIA Craig Jeffrey
MODERN IRELAND Senia Pašeta
MODERN ITALY Anna Cento Bull
MODERN JAPAN
    Christopher Goto-Jones
MODERN LATIN AMERICAN
    LITERATURE
    Roberto González Echevarría
MODERN WAR Richard English
MODERNISM Christopher Butler
MOLECULAR BIOLOGY Aysha Divan
    and Janice A. Royds
MOLECULES Philip Ball
MONASTICISM Stephen J. Davis
THE MONGOLS Morris Rossabi
MONTAIGNE William M. Hamlin
MOONS David A. Rothery
MORMONISM
    Richard Lyman Bushman
MOUNTAINS Martin F. Price
MUHAMMAD Jonathan A. C. Brown
MULTICULTURALISM Ali Rattansi
MULTILINGUALISM John C. Maher
MUSIC Nicholas Cook
MUSIC AND TECHNOLOGY Mark Katz
MYTH Robert A. Segal
NANOTECHNOLOGY Philip Moriarty
NAPOLEON David A. Bell
THE NAPOLEONIC WARS
    Mike Rapport
NATIONALISM Steven Grosby
NATIVE AMERICAN LITERATURE
    Sean Teuton
NAVIGATION Jim Bennett
NAZI GERMANY Jane Caplan
NEGOTIATION Carrie Menkel-Meadow
NEOLIBERALISM Manfred B. Steger
    and Ravi K. Roy
NETWORKS Guido Caldarelli and
    Michele Catanzaro
NEURODIVERSITY Robert Chapman
    and Sue Fletcher-Watson
THE NEW TESTAMENT
    Luke Timothy Johnson
THE NEW TESTAMENT AS
    LITERATURE Kyle Keefer
NEWTON Robert Iliffe
NIETZSCHE Michael Tanner
NINETEENTH-CENTURY BRITAIN
    Christopher Harvie and
    H. C. G. Matthew
THE NORMAN CONQUEST
    George Garnett
NORTH AMERICAN INDIANS
    Theda Perdue and Michael D. Green
NORTHERN IRELAND
    Marc Mulholland
NOTHING Frank Close
NUCLEAR PHYSICS Frank Close
NUCLEAR POWER Maxwell Irvine
NUCLEAR WEAPONS
    Joseph M. Siracusa
NUMBER THEORY Robin Wilson
NUMBERS Peter M. Higgins
NUTRITION David A. Bender
OBJECTIVITY Stephen Gaukroger
OBSERVATIONAL ASTRONOMY
    Geoff Cottrell
OCEANS Dorrik Stow
THE OLD TESTAMENT
    Michael D. Coogan
ORAL HISTORY Douglas A. Boyd
THE ORCHESTRA D. Kern Holoman
ORGANIC CHEMISTRY
    Graham Patrick
ORGANIZATIONS Mary Jo Hatch
ORGANIZED CRIME
    Georgios A. Antonopoulos and
    Georgios Papanicolaou
ORTHODOX CHRISTIANITY
    A. Edward Siecienski
OVID Llewelyn Morgan
PAGANISM Owen Davies
PAKISTAN Pippa Virdee
THE PALESTINIAN-ISRAELI
    CONFLICT Martin Bunton
PANDEMICS Christian W. McMillen
PARTICLE PHYSICS Frank Close
PAUL E. P. Sanders
IVAN PAVLOV Daniel P. Todes
PEACE Oliver P. Richmond
PENTECOSTALISM William K. Kay
PERCEPTION Brian Rogers
THE PERIODIC TABLE Eric R. Scerri
PHILOSOPHICAL METHOD
    Timothy Williamson

PHILOSOPHY Edward Craig
PHILOSOPHY IN THE ISLAMIC
    WORLD Peter Adamson
PHILOSOPHY OF BIOLOGY
    Samir Okasha
PHILOSOPHY OF LAW
    Raymond Wacks
PHILOSOPHY OF MIND
    Barbara Gail Montero
PHILOSOPHY OF PHYSICS
    David Wallace
PHILOSOPHY OF SCIENCE
    Samir Okasha
PHILOSOPHY OF RELIGION
    Tim Bayne
PHOTOGRAPHY Steve Edwards
PHYSICAL CHEMISTRY Peter Atkins
PHYSICS Sidney Perkowitz
PILGRIMAGE Ian Reader
PLAGUE Paul Slack
PLANETARY SYSTEMS
    Raymond T. Pierrehumbert
PLANETS David A. Rothery
PLANTS Timothy Walker
PLATE TECTONICS Peter Molnar
SYLVIA PLATH Heather Clark
PLATO Julia Annas
POETRY Bernard O'Donoghue
POLITICAL PHILOSOPHY David Miller
POLITICS Kenneth Minogue
POLYGAMY Sarah M. S. Pearsall
POPULISM Cas Mudde and
    Cristóbal Rovira Kaltwasser
POSTCOLONIALISM
    Robert J. C. Young
POSTMODERNISM Christopher Butler
POSTSTRUCTURALISM
    Catherine Belsey
POSTWAR EUROPE Richard Bessel
POVERTY Philip N. Jefferson
PREHISTORY Chris Gosden
PRESOCRATIC PHILOSOPHY
    Catherine Osborne
PRIVACY Raymond Wacks
PROBABILITY John Haigh
PROGRESSIVISM Walter Nugent
PROHIBITION W. J. Rorabaugh
PROJECTS Andrew Davies
PROTESTANTISM Mark A. Noll
MARCEL PROUST Joshua Landy
PSEUDOSCIENCE Michael D. Gordin
PSYCHIATRY Tom Burns
PSYCHOANALYSIS Daniel Pick
PSYCHOLINGUISTICS
    Ferenda Ferreria
PSYCHOLOGY Gillian Butler and
    Freda McManus
PSYCHOLOGY OF MUSIC
    Elizabeth Hellmuth Margulis
PSYCHOPATHY Essi Viding
PSYCHOTHERAPY Tom Burns and
    Eva Burns-Lundgren
PUBLIC ADMINISTRATION
    Stella Z. Theodoulou and Ravi K. Roy
PUBLIC HEALTH Virginia Berridge
PURITANISM Francis J. Bremer
THE QUAKERS Pink Dandelion
QUANTUM THEORY
    John Polkinghorne
RACISM Ali Rattansi
RADIOACTIVITY Claudio Tuniz
RASTAFARI Ennis B. Edmonds
READING Belinda Jack
THE REAGAN REVOLUTION Gil Troy
REALITY Jan Westerhoff
RECONSTRUCTION Allen C. Guelzo
THE REFORMATION Peter Marshall
REFUGEES Gil Loescher
RELATIVITY Russell Stannard
RELIGION Thomas A. Tweed
RELIGION IN AMERICA Timothy Beal
THE RENAISSANCE Jerry Brotton
RENAISSANCE ART
    Geraldine A. Johnson
RENEWABLE ENERGY Nick Jelley
REPTILES T. S. Kemp
REVOLUTIONS Jack A. Goldstone
RHETORIC Richard Toye
RISK Baruch Fischhoff and John Kadvany
RITUAL Barry Stephenson
RIVERS Nick Middleton
ROBOTICS Alan Winfield
ROCKS Jan Zalasiewicz
ROMAN BRITAIN Peter Salway
THE ROMAN EMPIRE
    Christopher Kelly
THE ROMAN REPUBLIC
    David M. Gwynn
ROMANTICISM Michael Ferber
ROUSSEAU Robert Wokler

THE RULE OF LAW Aziz Z. Huq
RUSSELL A. C. Grayling
THE RUSSIAN ECONOMY
    Richard Connolly
RUSSIAN HISTORY Geoffrey Hosking
RUSSIAN LITERATURE Catriona Kelly
RUSSIAN POLITICS Brian D. Taylor
THE RUSSIAN REVOLUTION
    S. A. Smith
SAINTS Simon Yarrow
SAMURAI Michael Wert
SAVANNAS Peter A. Furley
SCEPTICISM Duncan Pritchard
SCHIZOPHRENIA Chris Frith and
    Eve Johnstone
SCHOPENHAUER
    Christopher Janaway
SCIENCE AND RELIGION
    Thomas Dixon and Adam R. Shapiro
SCIENCE FICTION David Seed
THE SCIENTIFIC REVOLUTION
    Lawrence M. Principe
SCOTLAND Rab Houston
SECULARISM Andrew Copson
THE SELF Marya Schechtman
SEXUAL SELECTION Marlene Zuk and
    Leigh W. Simmons
SEXUALITY Véronique Mottier
WILLIAM SHAKESPEARE Stanley Wells
SHAKESPEARE'S COMEDIES
    Bart van Es
SHAKESPEARE'S SONNETS
    AND POEMS Jonathan F. S. Post
SHAKESPEARE'S TRAGEDIES
    Stanley Wells
GEORGE BERNARD SHAW
    Christopher Wixson
MARY SHELLEY Charlotte Gordon
THE SHORT STORY Andrew Kahn
SIKHISM Eleanor Nesbitt
SILENT FILM Donna Kornhaber
THE SILK ROAD James A. Millward
SLANG Jonathon Green
SLEEP Steven W. Lockley and
    Russell G. Foster
SMELL Matthew Cobb
ADAM SMITH Christopher J. Berry
SOCIAL AND CULTURAL
    ANTHROPOLOGY
    John Monaghan and Peter Just
SOCIALISM Michael Newman
SOCIAL PSYCHOLOGY Richard J. Crisp
SOCIAL SCIENCE Alexander Betts
SOCIAL WORK Sally Holland and
    Jonathan Scourfield
SOCIOLINGUISTICS John Edwards
SOCIOLOGY Steve Bruce
SOCRATES C. C. W. Taylor
SOFT MATTER Tom McLeish
SOPHOCLES Edith Hall
SOUND Mike Goldsmith
SOUTHEAST ASIA James R. Rush
THE SOVIET UNION Stephen Lovell
THE SPANISH CIVIL WAR
    Helen Graham
SPANISH LITERATURE Jo Labanyi
THE SPARTANS Andrew J. Bayliss
SPINOZA Roger Scruton
SPIRITUALITY Philip Sheldrake
SPORT Mike Cronin
STARS Andrew King
STATISTICS David J. Hand
STEM CELLS Jonathan Slack
STOICISM Brad Inwood
STRUCTURAL ENGINEERING
    David Blockley
STUART BRITAIN John Morrill
SUBURBS Carl Abbott
THE SUN Philip Judge
SUPERCONDUCTIVITY
    Stephen Blundell
SUPERSTITION Stuart Vyse
SURVEILLANCE David Lyon
SUSTAINABILITY Saleem H. Ali
SYMBIOSIS Nancy A. Moran
SYMMETRY Ian Stewart
SYNAESTHESIA Julia Simner
SYNTHETIC BIOLOGY Jamie A. Davies
SYSTEMS BIOLOGY Eberhard O. Voit
TAXATION Stephen Smith
TEETH Peter S. Ungar
TERRORISM Charles Townshend
THEATRE Marvin Carlson
THEOLOGY David F. Ford
THINKING AND REASONING
    Jonathan St B. T. Evans
HENRY DAVID THOREAU
    Lawrence Buell
THOUGHT Tim Bayne
THUCYDIDES Jennifer T. Roberts

TIBETAN BUDDHISM Matthew T. Kapstein
TIDES David George Bowers and Emyr Martyn Roberts
TIME Jenann Ismael
TOCQUEVILLE Harvey C. Mansfield
TOLERATION Andrew Murphy
J. R. R. TOLKIEN Matthew Townend
LEO TOLSTOY Liza Knapp
TOPOLOGY Richard Earl
TRAGEDY Adrian Poole
TRANSLATION Matthew Reynolds
THE TREATY OF VERSAILLES Michael S. Neiberg
TRIGONOMETRY Glen Van Brummelen
THE TROJAN WAR Eric H. Cline
ANTHONY TROLLOPE Dinah Birch
TRUST Katherine Hawley
THE TUDORS John Guy
TWENTIETH-CENTURY BRITAIN Kenneth O. Morgan
TYPOGRAPHY Paul Luna
THE UNITED NATIONS Jussi M. Hanhimäki
UNIVERSITIES AND COLLEGES David Palfreyman and Paul Temple
THE U.S. CIVIL WAR Louis P. Masur
THE U.S. CONGRESS Donald A. Ritchie
THE U.S. CONSTITUTION David J. Bodenhamer
THE U.S. SUPREME COURT Linda Greenhouse
UTILITARIANISM Katarzyna de Lazari-Radek and Peter Singer
UTOPIANISM Lyman Tower Sargent
VATICAN II Shaun Blanchard and Stephen Bullivant
VETERINARY SCIENCE James Yeates
THE VICTORIANS Martin Hewitt
THE VIKINGS Julian D. Richards
VIOLENCE Philip Dwyer
THE VIRGIN MARY Mary Joan Winn Leith
THE VIRTUES Craig A. Boyd and Kevin Timpe
VIRUSES Dorothy H. Crawford
VOLCANOES Michael J. Branney and Jan Zalasiewicz
VOLTAIRE Nicholas Cronk
WAR AND RELIGION Jolyon Mitchell and Joshua Rey
WAR AND TECHNOLOGY Alex Roland
WATER John Finney
WAVES Mike Goldsmith
WEATHER Storm Dunlop
SIMONE WEIL A. Rebecca Rozelle-Stone
THE WELFARE STATE David Garland
WITCHCRAFT Malcolm Gaskill
WITTGENSTEIN A. C. Grayling
WORK Stephen Fineman
WORLD MUSIC Philip Bohlman
WORLD MYTHOLOGY David Leeming
THE WORLD TRADE ORGANIZATION Amrita Narlikar
WORLD WAR II Gerhard L. Weinberg
WRITING AND SCRIPT Andrew Robinson
ZIONISM Michael Stanislawski
ÉMILE ZOLA Brian Nelson

Available soon:

THOMAS MORE Peter Marshall
DECISION MAKING Stefano Palminteri and Valentin Wyart

HUMANITARIANISM Julia F. Irwin

For more information visit our website

www.oup.com/vsi/

Stephen Thomson

ADMINISTRATIVE LAW

A Very Short Introduction

Great Clarendon Street, Oxford, OX2 6DP,
United Kingdom

Oxford University Press is a department of the University of Oxford.
It furthers the University's objective of excellence in research, scholarship,
and education by publishing worldwide. Oxford is a registered trade mark of
Oxford University Press in the UK and in certain other countries.

© Stephen Thomson 2025

The moral rights of the author have been asserted.

All rights reserved. No part of this publication may be reproduced, stored in a retrieval system, transmitted, used for text and data mining, or used for training artificial intelligence, in any form or by any means, without the prior permission in writing of Oxford University Press, or as expressly permitted by law, by licence or under terms agreed with the appropriate reprographics rights organization. Enquiries concerning reproduction outside the scope of the above should be sent to the Rights Department, Oxford University Press, at the address above.

You must not circulate this work in any other form
and you must impose this same condition on any acquirer.

Published in the United States of America by Oxford University Press
198 Madison Avenue, New York, NY 10016, United States of America

British Library Cataloguing in Publication Data

Data available

Library of Congress Control Number: 2025947612

ISBN 9780198882176

DOI: 10.1093/9780191991295.001.0001

Printed and bound by
CPI Group (UK) Ltd., Croydon, CR0 4YY

The manufacturer's authorised representative in the EU for product safety is
Oxford University Press España S.A. of Parque Empresarial San Fernando de Henares,
Avenida de Castilla, 2 – 28830 Madrid (www.oup.es/en or product.safety@oup.com).
OUP España S.A. also acts as importer into Spain of products made by the manufacturer.

Links to third party websites are provided by Oxford in good faith and
for information only. Oxford disclaims any responsibility for the materials
contained in any third party website referenced in this work.

For Benjamin

Contents

Acknowledgements xix

List of illustrations xxi

1 What is administrative law? 1

2 Internal review 15

3 Administrative tribunals 24

4 Judicial review 33

5 From ombudsmen to public inquiries: Other administrative law controls 69

6 The future of administrative law 101

References 113

Further reading 119

Index 123

Acknowledgements

I would like to express my thanks to various people who have contributed their time and support in bringing this book to fruition. I am grateful to Eric C. Ip for encouraging me to write this book in the first place. My thanks are due to Michael Asimow, David Blincow, Matthew Groves, and Greg Weeks for offering valuable comments on drafts of the manuscript, and to Paul Daly for helpful answers to various questions. I am also grateful to Oxford University Press for supporting this project, in particular Latha Menon, Luciana O'Flaherty, and Imogene Haslam, and to the anonymous reviewers who gave the proposal a positive appraisal. I would also like to gratefully acknowledge those people who have over the years helped to inspire and shape my views on administrative law and the relationship between the individual and the state.

Of course, I am responsible for any errors in the text and the views expressed are my own.

List of illustrations

1. A Royal Commission into the Robodebt Scheme hearing room, Brisbane, Australia **10**
   Alamy

2. Sir Humphrey Appleby: Smug, redoubtable, and a more permanent feature of government than his elected minister **12**
   Shutterstock

3. A prison van operated by private company Serco: one of many examples at the interface of the public and private sectors **40**
   Alamy

4. Lord Diplock was one of the most influential English judges of the 20th century and more broadly on judicial review in the common law world **45**
   Alamy

5. The former Gaumont Cinema in Wednesbury, West Midlands, UK; the unlikely subject of one of the most well-known rules of judicial review in the common law world **60**
   https://cinema-theatre.org.uk/our-campaigns/cinemas-at-risk/gaumont-wednesbury/

6. Hillary Clinton appears before the US House Select Committee on Events Surrounding the 2012 Terrorist Attack in Benghazi, Washington, DC, USA **78**
   Shutterstock

7. Paula Vennells, former chief executive officer of Post Office Ltd, appears before the Post Office Horizon IT Inquiry in London, UK **80**
   https://www.postofficehorizoninquiry.org.uk/hearings/phases-56-23-may-2024

8 Praveen Kumar Srivastava is sworn in as the Central Vigilance Commissioner, New Delhi, India **88**
https://pib.gov.in/ShowAlbum.aspx?albumid=141991&reg=3&lang=1

9 A Virtual Crown Court mock trial piloted by the UK charity JUSTICE in the early days of the COVID-19 pandemic **106**
Alamy

Chapter 1
What is administrative law?

In September 1990, a young child in Cambridgeshire, UK, was diagnosed with non-Hodgkins lymphoma and lymphoblastic leukaemia. A round of chemotherapy was completed with apparent success. However, in December 1993, the child developed acute myeloid leukaemia and was treated with a second round of chemotherapy, radiotherapy, and a bone marrow transplant. Sadly, there was a relapse of the acute myeloid leukaemia and there was medical opinion to the effect that the child would be likely only to live for a further six to eight weeks and that further treatment would not be useful. There was also medical opinion to the effect that there was some, albeit a low 10 per cent, probability of success in a further—third—round of chemotherapy costing around £15,000 and, if successful, followed by a second bone marrow transplant costing around £60,000. The public health authority for the area, Cambridge Health Authority, refused to fund this additional treatment due to its experimental nature, relevant medical opinion, and the limited resources available. The family of the young child was understandably distraught.

The family applied for judicial review of the Health Authority's decision in a case known as *R v Cambridge Health Authority, ex parte B* [1995] EWCA Civ 43. The case was heard in the Queen's Bench Division of the High Court. The family 'won'—the judge ruled that the authority could not simply 'toll the bell of tight resources' and had failed to 'explain the priorities that have led them to decline to fund the treatment'. A glimmer of hope for the family and the prospects of the child living. But the Health Authority appealed against the judgment. The appeal was heard in the Court of Appeal where the three judges took a different view. With every sympathy expressed for the family's desperate situation, the judges explained that in a world of finite resources the Health Authority was entitled to reach the decision that it did. The court felt that this kind of resource allocation question was ultimately not a legal question. The authority had taken into consideration all that it was legally entitled to and had not exceeded its legal powers in a way that would allow the court to intervene. The door slammed shut for the family: no more state-funded medical treatment for the young child. The child died in May 1996.

This was an administrative law case. Not all cases in this field are matters of life and death, but this vividly illustrates how dramatic and consequential this area of law can be. We may not realize it, but we all regularly come into contact with administrative law. Whether we are paying our taxes, enrolling our children in a state school, applying for a licence to run a restaurant, claiming welfare benefits, or even complaining to a local authority about refuse collection, we are engaging with administrative law. Many of us are employed by public sector organizations, from government departments to publicly run schools and universities, and that also engages elements of administrative law. In short, whenever we come into contact with the state we are probably interacting with this area of law. And if the examples just given sound mundane, it is good to bear in mind the *Cambridge Health Authority* case and also some major issues that have affected many or most of us, wherever we might be: whether Brexit in the UK, Robodebt in Australia, counter-terrorism controls in the wake of the September 11 terrorist attacks in the USA, the Sabarimala verdict in India, the anti-mask law during the 2019–20 Hong Kong riots, or the imposition of COVID-19 lockdown and quarantine regulations globally, administrative law has played a key role in these events and many more besides.

The first question is, therefore, what exactly is administrative law? This is not so straightforward to define because it often blends into other areas of law, like constitutional law and human rights law, and because parts of some areas of law—like immigration law, planning law, and taxation law—are in large part specialized aspects of administrative law. The subject is also heavily conditioned by politics, from government policies on immigration to ministerial intervention when a corruption scandal comes to light. But let us start with the name: what is 'administrative' about this area of law? This is a reference to the administration of the state, in other words how the state and public sector operates. Public sector decision makers are largely seen as 'administrators' in this context, administering legal powers they have been given, usually by parliaments and sometimes by constitutions, when they make decisions about almost anything from immigration, housing, licensing, and planning to taxation, education, health, policing, and public procurement. Often we refer to these administrators as 'decision makers' or 'public officials'; this book tends to use the term 'decision makers'. Administrative law is all about what these decision makers can and cannot do; but that would be to set the definitional net too broadly because other areas of law—like constitutional law, contract law, and the law of negligence—also impose their own obligations on decision makers.

We can begin to narrow down the definition of administrative law by saying that it is a branch of public law. Whereas private law regulates 'horizontal' relationships between people, companies, and organizations, such as in contract law, tort law, and property law, public law regulates 'vertical' relationships between individuals and the state. In short, the state can do things to us that we cannot do to the state or to each other. It can arrest us, imprison us, deport us, tax us, license our activities, close our businesses and schools—we cannot do these things. With these special powers come special obligations, and that is where public law comes into play, as it is fundamentally concerned with the special obligations that apply to the state in its dealings with individuals. This is not a completely clear-cut definition, because we can enter into contracts with the state (those of us employed by the state are an obvious example) and the state can be liable to pay us damages for negligence. But those are still considered to be private law obligations, because we can all contract with each other, we can all be liable in negligence to each other, and so on. There is also a 'horizontal' dimension to public law relationships, like when government officials respond to freedom of information (FOI) requests (which is a legal requirement imposed by the legislature) or are called to give evidence before a public inquiry (also a legal requirement imposed by the legislature), but the horizontal versus vertical distinction still helps us to understand the basic nature of this area of law and how it is different from others. Public law is fundamentally concerned with those things that only the state can do. Administrative law is a key part of public law.

We can break administrative law down into two main aspects. First, who applies and enforces administrative law? Second, what are the substantive rules of administrative law? The first question informs the structure of this book, because the chapters are broadly divided by the institutions that apply and enforce administrative law. When we want to have an administrative decision reviewed, there is a range of bodies that we can approach. The first step is to ask the government department or public body that made the decision to reconsider—this is called internal review and forms the subject of Chapter 2. We do not actually know as much about internal review as we do about other forms of control because many of these complaints never make it into the public domain. But we can usually take our complaint elsewhere. Legislation often gives us a right to appeal to an administrative tribunal (the subject of Chapter 3) which, as we shall see, looks and feels a bit like a court, but is not a court. If our complaint is about the legality of a decision or decision-making process, rather than a broader complaint about standards or fairness, then we can go to a court to seek judicial review—the subject of Chapter 4. But there is a myriad of other bodies that we can approach with our complaint about an administrative decision depending on what has happened and the nature of the complaint. These include ombudsmen, parliamentary complaints procedures, parliamentary and congressional committees, public inquiries, human rights monitors, anti-corruption bodies, public service integrity bodies, financial integrity and public audit bodies, regulators, and FOI bodies. Some of these might conduct administrative review without us even lodging a complaint. These bodies are the subject of Chapter 5. Each of these channels for challenging decisions could and frequently do occupy books much longer than this one, so by necessity we can only cover the basics and the main areas of administrative law at that. But we can already see that although 'administrative law' sounds quite niche, perhaps narrow, it is in fact a vast area of law with many moving parts.

The substantive rules of administrative law are as varied as they are extensive. They are easiest (but by no means easy) to pin down in the law of judicial review, where court judgments are often publicly available and the courts apply a fairly consistent set of rules, albeit rules of some complexity. But a lot of administrative law is more elusive. Sometimes this is because the enforcing institution does not use a system of precedent (where earlier decisions to some extent dictate future decisions); a prominent example would be administrative tribunals which, for reasons explained in Chapter 3, can do certain things that courts cannot when making decisions. Sometimes the rules of administrative law are elusive because the institution does not enforce rules as such. An excellent example is ombudsmen, which tend to make recommendations in line with values or principles rather than rules; much of their work is informal and non-adversarial in nature. Some areas of administrative law are largely concealed from public view: internal review is a great example. This process can take many different shapes and forms across institutions and legal systems, and much of what goes on in this regard is not even made public, thus it is difficult to articulate 'rules' of administrative law in this context. But, again, we are getting a sense of how vast an area is administrative law.

Of course, it was not always this vast. Administrative law has grown in pace with the growth of the administrative state. In a country like the UK, this process started in earnest in the mid-19th century as local, regional, and national infrastructure took shape—roads, railways, harbours, water systems, inspection committees, taxation frameworks, and the like. Legislation often gave powers to boards and commissions which took binding decisions in these areas, and administrative law needed to respond to the growth of their powers with rules about what decisions they could make and the processes by which they could be made. Take, for example, the famous English case of *Cooper v Wandsworth Board of Works* (1863) 143 ER 414. Legislation stated that, before a person shall begin to build a new house, they shall give seven days' notice to the district board of their intention to build. If that notice had not been given, the district board was empowered to demolish the house. The court decided that, although the individual in the case had failed to give this notice and was in the course of building the house, the district board had to give him an opportunity to be heard before deciding to proceed with the demolition. This was, the court reasoned, because there could be many different reasons for notice having not been given and that the district board must consider the reason for notice having not been given before proceeding with a demolition. Essentially, the legislation gave the district board broad powers but the courts trimmed them back by imposing this procedural fairness requirement. Parliament had given the district board considerable administrative power, but the courts developed an administrative law qualification on how that power could be exercised.

The growth of administrative law was particularly acute in the 20th century as the welfare state and systems for licensing, planning, regulation, local administration, and immigration grew and multiplied. With those burgeoning systems of administration have come burgeoning rules and procedures for control. The state grows and with it grows administrative law: in the English case of *Ridge v Baldwin* [1964] AC 40, the judge Lord Reid stated that '[w]e do not have a developed system of administrative law, perhaps because until fairly recently we did not need it'. Nowadays, administrative law covers a vast and diverse range of decision makers from prime ministers, executive agency heads, and national healthcare authorities to local police forces, education authorities, and council officials. Frequent targets of administrative law challenges are immigration, housing, licensing, and planning decision makers, but really any public sector body or official (with some exceptions in the areas of defence and national security) is subject to the controls of administrative law.

Administrative law bursts into public notoriety more frequently than many people appreciate. Public inquiries are a good example of this—many people in the UK have heard of and know something about the Iraq Inquiry, the Grenfell Tower Inquiry, the Manchester Arena Inquiry, the Post Office Horizon IT Inquiry, and the UK COVID-19 Inquiry. So are parliamentary and congressional committees: everyone has heard of the Watergate scandal and Hillary Clinton deleting emails from a private server which impeded the work of the US House Select Committee on Events Surrounding the 2012 Terrorist Attack in Benghazi. Many enjoyed the spectacle of George Galloway MP tearing into a bemused Senator Norm Coleman at the Senate Permanent Subcommittee on Investigations on alleged abuses of the United Nations' (UN's) Oil-for-Food Program. Whistleblowers like W. Mark Felt ('Deep Throat'), Chelsea Manning, and Edward Snowden are household names. All of these are, front and centre, examples of administrative law in action.

Of course, it is not all the stuff of newspaper front pages. Some of the biggest rules in administrative law emerged from cases with very banal facts, such as a case about under-15s being admitted to a cinema on a Sunday (*Associated Provincial Picture Houses Ltd v Wednesbury Corporation* [1948] 1 KB 223), or a case about milk producers requesting that a government minister appoint a committee to investigate regional differences in milk pricing (*Padfield v Minister for Agriculture, Fisheries and Food* [1968] AC 997 (HL)), or a case about a company complaining about a financial regulator's handling of another company's rule breach (*R v Panel on Take-overs and Mergers, ex parte Datafin* [1987] QB 815). These are issues that are unlikely to keep many people awake at night, but the resultant rules of administrative law are more relevant to them than they realize. When a person is refused medical treatment by a public health authority, or is unsuccessful in an application for public housing, or has a refugee application rejected, or rides in a taxi without properly working seatbelts, or receives an erroneous tax demand, or suddenly has extra conditions added to their business licence, or is excluded from their university course, or is required to show evidence of vaccination or a negative antigen test before entering a public building—these situations are the bread and butter of administrative law and a person subject to these rules and decisions would benefit greatly from a working knowledge of it.

Sometimes it will be the case that a government official has got an individual decision wrong. Other times there will be a large-scale systemic failure of public administration which causes widespread injustice. Administrative law can then step in with a menu of options for tackling those injustices and preventing a repeat.

A good example is the Robodebt saga in Australia. Before the programme was introduced by the Abbott government in 2016, recipients of social welfare payments that were deemed to have been overpaid had manual calculations applied to determine what should be repaid. Robodebt was a programme which determined overpayments and issued debt recovery notices on an automated basis. Numerous problems existed with the scheme, including the issuance of notices for debts that either did not exist or were lower than claimed, difficulties associated with disputing those debts, and shifting the burden of proof from the agency which disburses Australian social welfare payments to prove that the debt was due, to benefits recipients to prove that the debt was not due. Hundreds of thousands of people were affected by the scandal, particularly some of the poorest in society.

Administrative law played a pivotal role in bringing the programme to an end (though some administrative law processes were more effective than others, and some actually slowed down the process of termination). Unusually, this involved numerous aspects of administrative law—an administrative tribunal, judicial review, an ombudsman, two parliamentary inquiries, and a commission of inquiry to name just the main moving parts. The Commonwealth Ombudsman issued a report in 2017 which made several recommendations including that the application of a 10 per cent recovery fee should be manually reassessed in the context of the customer's personal circumstances, improved clarity in communications with customers, and improved assistance to vulnerable customers. Two parliamentary inquiries, beginning in 2017 and 2019 respectively, recommended among other things that the scheme should be put on hold until procedural fairness flaws were addressed, that manual reassessments of debt be made in particular cases, and that a Royal Commission (the highest level of commission of inquiry in Australia) be established by the government to investigate the scheme. That Royal Commission was duly established and reported in July 2023—the report is over 1,000 pages long and it made numerous recommendations. Robodebt was terminated as a scheme on 30 June 2020 under the Morrison government, concluding what a judge in the case of *Prygodicz v Commonwealth of Australia (No 2)* [2021] FCA 634 called 'a shameful chapter in the administration of the Commonwealth social security system and a massive failure of public administration'. Administrative law was the forum in which that failure was identified and the scheme terminated.

1. A Royal Commission into the Robodebt Scheme hearing room, Brisbane, Australia.

Though administrative law has many applications and players, there are a number of core values of so-called 'good administration' and 'good governance' that tie much of the field together, at least in the common law countries. These include legality, consistency, rationality, evidence-based decision making, accountability, transparency, due process, fairness, impartiality, open-mindedness, and efficiency. If the work of courts, tribunals, ombudsmen, public inquiries, and all the other institutions of administrative law could be boiled down to their common denominators, the list would look something like this. Some of these values are encapsulated in the 'Seven Principles of Public Life', also known as the 'Nolan Principles', which were adopted in the UK in 1994 to apply to members of the legislature, executive, and judiciary. These are (i) selflessness, (ii) integrity, (iii) objectivity, (iv) accountability, (v) openness, (vi) honesty, and (vii) leadership. Similarly, Australia applies certain 'values' to its public service, namely (i) impartiality, (ii) commitment to service, (iii) accountability, (iv) respectfulness, and (v) ethicality.

This book is focused on common law countries/jurisdictions like the UK, Ireland, US, Canada, Australia, New Zealand, India, and Hong Kong for two reasons. First, civil law countries like France, Germany, Italy, and Japan generally have a different system of administrative law, though they often have a number of the same or similar institutions like tribunals and ombudsmen, and are often upholding similar values to those just described. Second, more authoritarian legal systems are largely excluded from the scope of this book. Countries like China, Russia, and North Korea do have administrative law and to a greater or lesser extent have some similar administrative law institutions but, as countries with poor democratic and rule of law credentials, administrative law is often a tool for confirming and consolidating centralized, authoritarian power rather than securing accountability in the orthodox sense. This is something of an oversimplification of the role of administrative law in those countries, but it is sufficient for a work of this nature to note that they are too different to merit discussion in the same book and in the same context.

While administrative law might at first sound like quite a narrow or niche subject, it is already obvious that that is not the case. It touches on and overlaps with other important areas like constitutional law, human rights law, counter-terrorism law, data privacy law, cyber-security law, anti-money laundering law, taxation law, immigration law, planning law, licensing law, public procurement law, telecommunications and broadcasting law, education law, pensions law, discrimination and equalities law, state secrets law, public health law, and many more besides. Clearly these areas can only be mentioned in passing but the reader should be aware of their relevance to the subject of administrative law, and how the fundamental principles of administrative law tie many of these subjects together. The breadth of this collection of related areas only underscores how central administrative law is to the daily operation of the public sector and the importance of a proper understanding of it to public officials and anyone who comes into contact with the state.

It should also be clear why administrative law plays a vital role in securing accountability in the public sector and why there is such a need for this kind of accountability in the first place. Since the political ascendancy of Donald Trump there has been much made of the term 'deep state' and, if considered in a less conspiratorial manner than that in which it is usually mentioned, it can be understood what the basic idea is getting at even if its expression is clearly overblown. Readers familiar with the timeless BBC sitcom *Yes Minister* will recognize the resistant role that Permanent Secretary Sir Humphrey Appleby plays in grinding down his government minister (Jim Hacker) whenever the minister tries to do anything. It is clear from the plot that Appleby is running the show as much as, or perhaps even more than,

2. Sir Humphrey Appleby: Smug, redoubtable, and a more permanent feature of government than his elected minister.

Hacker, although it is Hacker who is the elected politician and who must answer to the public.

Steve Hilton, a former director of strategy to UK Prime Minister David Cameron, claimed that Cameron once said of the civil service: 'You cannot underestimate how much they believe it's their job to actually run the country and to resist the changes put forward by people they dismiss as "here today, gone tomorrow" politicians.' While the minister would typically be politically accountable and removable through elections, the permanent secretary and other civil servants must instead be held accountable through other channels. That is the domain of administrative law. (For the record, this is not to pretend that politicians are pure servants of their constituents who are an unequivocally noble check on a self-interested bureaucracy.)

There is one final chapter in the book, Chapter 6, which considers the future of administrative law. Though it has been with us in some form or another since the modern state emerged, administrative law as we know it is under threat and the cracks are beginning to show. From public bodies running out of money to public health and environmental emergencies, and from artificial intelligence and automation in government decision making to political instability and waning public trust in government institutions, the existing rules, processes, and institutions of administrative law face many challenges. Administrative law has historically grown from, and adapted to, changes in government. The difference now is that administrative law as we currently know it might be incapable of adapting properly to these challenges. When we transfer decision-making functions from government officials to computers, do we really know what we are doing and understand the potential consequences? When public bodies are becoming so resource constrained that they can barely carry out their statutory functions, what can a court, tribunal, or ombudsman really do about that? When we suspend the ordinary controls of administrative law during pandemics and other emergencies, can we be sure that the costs we are imposing on legal and political accountability are not causing more harm than the ones they are designed to mitigate? We consider some of these imposing challenges for administrative law in Chapter 6 to round off our discussion.

Chapter 2
Internal review

One of the most important aspects of administrative law is virtually hidden from public view. That makes any discussion or commentary of it fairly difficult, yet it is a key process within the subject area. We are dealing with internal review, namely processes internal to the department or body being complained about whereby the decision can be challenged or reviewed. Many of those internal reviews will be successful and result in a changed decision, and unless the department publishes that information voluntarily or is obliged to do so under legislation or through a freedom of information (FOI) request (for example, in statistical form), then we might never hear about those cases. Many others will be unsuccessful, but the person who complained will not have the time, resources, energy, or knowledge required to challenge the decision in a more formal setting such as a court or tribunal. We might also never hear of those cases. Only a small minority of unsuccessful internal reviews would lead to the aggrieved person taking their case to a court or tribunal, or indeed to traditional or social media, the first time we would be likely to have any knowledge of its existence; so the vast majority of complaints about administrative decisions probably never see the public light of day in the first place.

Some bodies will have more formalized internal review processes, for example a designated officer or panel, separate from the original decision maker, whose task it is to receive and process requests for internal review. Others will have less formalized processes, for example the official who made the original decision is approached and informally asked to change their mind—and they might agree to do so. In fact, they might be approached not even by the person affected by the decision, but by a manager in the government department who is concerned about the appearance or ramifications of a decision. The public would be none the wiser. Given the wide range of internal review processes across public bodies generally, let alone public bodies in different countries, it is difficult to make generalizations about how internal review works. This is again exacerbated by the fact that much of this exercise may be informal and/or concealed from public view. However, it is important to note that we are dealing here with processes that can result in changed decisions, not general complaints handling which is broader in scope and can include issues of service delivery or organizational performance with ill-defined, possibly no, potential for changed decisions. The primary objective of internal review is to ensure that the decision taken is 'correct' in terms of the applicable law, procedure, policy, and the merits of the individual case.

There are clearly advantages to internal review for both the complainant and the decision maker. The complainant will probably have to spend little or no money in the course of making their complaint. It might be as straightforward as picking up the phone and asking the body to reconsider their decision or clicking on a link in an email. A lot of the time and money consumed by more formal external review processes like judicial review and tribunal review will likely be avoided. Egregious errors like basic factual mistakes or bias stand a good chance of being picked up. The commission of legal errors might also be picked up if internal reviewers are sufficiently legally trained—it is insightful to note survey responses from internal review officers in a report of the Australian Administrative Review Council where a recurring theme was the increasing complexity of legislation and policy, and a lack of legal understanding and training on the part of primary decision makers. Even if the decision is not changed at internal review, the individual may feel listened to and that they were given another chance. The decision maker may also benefit. They might not have to defend their decision in a court or tribunal, with all the expense and human resource that that requires (not forgetting that defending the decision ultimately requires committing more public resources to the matter). It may also facilitate a more cooperative or non-combative mindset on the part of the public authority, learning from their experience or improving the quality of their decision making rather than entering the adversarial arena of litigation where it can, for various reasons, be difficult to back down. Public embarrassment or reputational damage for the public authority might also be avoided. It will in most situations be the lowest cost way to resolve disputes for both complainant and decision maker, and the lowest cost for the public purse.

There are drawbacks, however. The first is the potential for inconsistent treatment of complaints when the reviewing official is different across review requests. Near-identical complaints might even be treated differently based on the luck of the draw. If the public authority has engaged in some kind of illegality in making the original decision, there is the possibility for that illegality to be repeated or exacerbated during the internal review process, perhaps even in a way that wrongly persuades the complainant that there was no illegality in the original decision-making process. Public authorities might also try to use internal review processes as a way to discourage complainants from taking their complaint to an external body like a court or tribunal. This could occur in a number of ways, from misleading complainants about their likelihood of success in using an external body to simply slowing down the whole dispute so that the complainant runs out of time, patience, or options and increasing the likelihood that they just give up. In fact, any legal requirement to use an internal review process before being allowed to take the matter to a court or tribunal might add to the complainant's costs and sense of injustice, if it is simply a formality which is unlikely to result in a changed or improved decision; in other words a step that simply has to be gone through before being able to have the matter considered by a judge or tribunal member. The relative absence from public view of what happens in internal review processes is both a blessing and a curse.

The existence of internal review mechanisms is not, however, completely hidden from public view. They might, for example, be referenced in government departments' annual reports. In the UK, certain immigration decisions made by the Home Office which are alleged to be wrong due to a case working error can be referred for internal review (which is termed an 'administrative review') under the Immigration Rules (Appendix AR: Administrative Review). The review can be requested while within the UK, at the UK border, or outside the UK. There is a fee of £80 for an internal review which is usually refunded only if the application is rejected as invalid or the decision which was challenged is changed. The review is conducted by a different official on a team independent from the one that made the original decision. If the error is successfully established, the decision can be withdrawn or amended. If applicable, the Home Office will not remove the applicant from the UK while the internal review is pending.

Internal reviews for a visa decision can be subject to long delays. It can take 28 days or longer to receive the result of the review if the visa was cancelled at the border, six months or longer to receive the result if inside the UK, and 12 months or longer to receive the result if outside the UK. While the Home Office states that 'your rights are not affected by the delay in processing applications', such lengthy delays can obviously result in a huge amount of uncertainty and even cost for an applicant. People are, ultimately, trying to live their lives and the need for the review might be the result of an actual error committed by the Home Office in the first place. If the application for internal review is unsuccessful, the original decision will stand, which might include requiring the applicant to leave the UK, unless they take their case to a tribunal or court.

A different example from England is the right under the Housing Act 1996 to internal review of most homelessness decisions made by local authorities. Interestingly, the authority has the statutory right to contract out its review process, but it can choose to run it internally. Again, the person who conducts the review cannot be the person who made the original decision, and the applicant must be notified of the review decision within a period of 3–12 weeks depending on the nature of the request for internal review. A person who had a right to request internal review can only apply to the county court 'on a point of law' (i.e. not on a factual or merits matter) if they are not satisfied with the outcome of the internal review decision or if that decision was not made within the specified time limits. In other words, if a person's complaint relates to a matter which is eligible for reconsideration under the internal review procedure, they *cannot* apply to the county court *unless* they first avail themselves of the internal review procedure. That procedure is then a barrier between the original decision being made and appealing to the county court. Judicial review (which is different from an appeal process, as explained in Chapter 4) is also not available where the person had a right to apply for internal review and did not use it. Clearly internal review is relatively formalized in this example and not just a case of the aggrieved person approaching the original decision maker and asking, 'Will you please change your mind?'

Other similar examples can be found. Following the enactment of the Welfare Reform Act 2012, a benefits claimant who is dissatisfied with a benefits decision must apply for 'mandatory reconsideration' by the Department for Work and Pensions (DWP) or His Majesty's Revenue and Customs (HMRC) before they are allowed to appeal to an independent tribunal called the First-tier Tribunal. This was a change to the previous system whereby a claimant could appeal against the benefits decision directly to a tribunal. Figures released by the DWP show that around 80 per cent of mandatory reconsiderations are unsuccessful. That, added to the fact that the number of tribunal appeals reduced following the introduction of this additional mandatory step, suggests that a number of claimants are giving up at the mandatory reconsideration stage. Even if an initial benefits decision is clearly wrong, the claimant cannot break free from the department that made it and must go through this additional stage before it can be considered by an independent tribunal. Some will of course be successful at the reconsideration stage—around 20 per cent—but for the rest, the period of time before they can have the decision considered by an independent tribunal is longer due to this additional mandatory internal review. While the successful 20 per cent would probably regard the internal review process as effective, the unsuccessful 80 per cent probably would not. The First-tier Tribunal is clearly not going to regard all 80 per cent of those decisions as wrongly decided, but it is interesting to note that the success rate in the independent tribunal is two to three times higher than at internal review. There can be many plausible reasons for this but it does raise the question of whether the introduction of a mandatory internal review stage was a positive development.

Internal reviews are also found in the area of FOI. A person whose FOI request is refused under the UK's Freedom of Information Act 2000 (see Chapter 5 for more discussion) must apply for internal review where a public body has an internal review process, before being allowed to appeal to the Information Commissioner. In Australia, a person who makes an FOI request and under which access is denied has a statutory right under the Freedom of Information Act 1982 to apply for internal review of the decision. The agency which made the decision must then issue a fresh decision within 30 days and that decision must be made by a different person from the one who made the original decision. There are no charges or fees for making the application for internal review. While this right to apply for internal review is secured in legislation, the actual process of reconsideration is not spelled out.

One country where internal review has quite a different flavour is the US. Other common law countries like the UK, Australia, and Canada mainly use external tribunals to hear appeals against administrative decisions. That is not to say that internal review is not used in those countries—we have already seen that it is—but that formal appeals against administrative decisions mainly lie to external bodies. That is not the case in the US, where the model is mostly based on 'executive agencies'. These agencies, which are branches of the government, make regulations which are published in the *Federal Register*. But they also prosecute breaches of those regulations and the applicable legislation. These 'rule-making' and 'adjudication' functions are seen as two sides of the agency coin. Disputes are generally decided by the agency itself in a formal adversarial hearing, and the same agency reconsiders the decision from that hearing. As a result, one leading US administrative lawyer, Michael Asimow, has referred to these agencies as 'combined-function agencies' because they combine the functions of investigation, prosecution, initial decision making, and reconsideration.

These combined-function agencies might sound odd. They certainly sound odd to administrative lawyers in other countries. How can the agency make a rule, then a decision on an adjudication of that rule, and then decide an appeal from that with any kind of impartiality or independence? Much of this process is governed by legislation called the Administrative Procedure Act of 1946. The Act provides various impartiality requirements for the officials who preside over these adversarial hearings, who are called 'Administrative Law Judges' (ALJs). (The idea of using the term 'judges' for decision makers in the executive branch also sounds odd to administrative lawyers elsewhere, not least in a system like the US which has quite a strict constitutional separation of powers between the legislative, executive, and judicial branches.) ALJs are structurally separated from other parts of the agency and enjoy tenure for life in a similar way to judges—i.e. they cannot be removed from post for making decisions that the agency does not like. This is underlined by the concept of 'justice without fear or favour', meaning that decisions are made without fear of reprisal for making an undesirable decision and without receiving favour for making a desirable decision.

However, the US Supreme Court held in the 2024 case of *Securities and Exchange Commission v Jarkesy*, No. 22-859, that Securities and Exchange Commission ALJs who imposed punitive civil penalties on defendants in the absence of a jury were in violation of the Seventh Amendment to the US Constitution, which guarantees the right to a jury trial in certain types of case. This groundbreaking decision has thrown into doubt the constitutionality of ALJs imposing civil penalties in other federal agencies. It is also worth noting that the *Jarkesy* case was followed by another landmark administrative law decision of the US Supreme Court the next day, in *Loper Bright Enterprises v Raimondo*, 603 US 369, which also weakens the position of executive agencies. The court in *Loper* overruled the principle of '*Chevron* deference' which required the courts in certain circumstances to defer to 'permissible' agency interpretations of statutes, even when the court interpreted the statute differently. *Loper* instead held that courts must exercise their own independent judgment in deciding whether an agency has acted within the limits of its statutory authority, and that courts may not defer to an agency interpretation of the law simply because a statute is ambiguous.

Not all of the aforementioned agency adjudicators are ALJs and not all decisions are made under the Administrative Procedure Act, and agency decisions can ultimately be challenged using judicial review, but structured internal review clearly plays a more prominent part in US administrative law than in other countries. ALJs, subject to what has just been said about the *Jarkesy* and *Loper* cases, nevertheless have more structural independence than the officials who typically conduct internal reviews in other countries. A further difference is that in other countries there is often an appeal to an external tribunal which, as we will understand from Chapter 3, is not necessarily just a legal complaint, but could be a complaint about the merits of the decision. Legal complaints can be dealt with by judicial review (see Chapter 4) in these other countries and also in the US, but a key difference is that the US does not usually offer the possibility of an *appeal* to an external tribunal, at least at the federal level. There are some exceptions such as in the fields of taxation and occupational safety and health, but these are indeed exceptions rather than the rule.

It can therefore be seen that there are benefits to having an internal review channel. It gives individuals an additional opportunity to have their decision reconsidered and is usually cheap or free of charge. But these internal review processes will not always work for the intended objective and could be used by government departments and public agencies to slow down the grievance process or discourage the individual from taking the matter further. A sizeable chunk of applicants will simply be ground down or give up. There are also questions about whether these internal review processes should be optional or mandatory; that choice will have further impacts on the behaviours and resources of both the organization and the individual. If an internal review process is established *instead* of making available an appeal to an external tribunal, as is often the case in the US, there are serious questions about what this does to administrative fairness and justice as experienced by the individual and whether they have a genuine opportunity to have the original decision overturned. Nevertheless, internal review clearly plays an important role in allowing for administrative decisions to be challenged.

Chapter 3
Administrative tribunals

In 2024 I co-edited a book entitled *Administrative Tribunals in the Common Law World* which brought together some of the leading scholars in this field. As we said in our introduction to the book: 'It is indeed a paradox of such a major international collaboration on tribunals that this book cannot—or will not—produce a global definition of a tribunal; though that difficulty has only been confirmed and compounded by the many experienced contributors to this volume.'

Examples from the book were Hugh Corder's statement that 'tribunals in South Africa take many forms, function in a myriad ways, and have radically varying levels of workload, efficiency, and effectiveness'; Guy Seidman's statement that the 'definition of what constitutes [a tribunal] is vague as is the precise number of entities that currently operate as [tribunals]' in Israel; and my own conclusion that my initial attempt to come up with a definitive list of tribunals in Hong Kong was futile.

The fact is that it is much more difficult to offer a concise definition of a tribunal than many other institutions of administrative law. It is often said that tribunals look and operate like courts, but fundamentally they are not courts. Tribunals are usually more specialized than courts in the sense that they tend to be set up to deal with disputes in particular areas, for example specialist immigration, taxation, or housing tribunals. They are fora in which individuals affected by government decisions can challenge them by way of appeal—the tribunal will often have the power to confirm the original decision (for example, a deportation order or the rejection of an application for public housing) or to change the decision. The instinctive response may be that this sounds like the work of a court, but that would be wrong.

The reason for this is subtle but vitally important. Courts consider issues of legality—nothing more. They are, after all, courts of *law*. If a person challenges a government decision in a court, they can only win the case if they prove that the government's decision was unlawful. If their complaint relates to anything else, for example whether the decision was inefficient, foolish, or hypocritical, the court cannot consider the application because these are (usually) not matters of law. We describe these as relating to the 'merits' of the case. Courts cannot consider the merits of government decisions because the constitutional separation of powers rule tells us that while courts decide legal disputes, they cannot decide matters of policy because that is for the executive branch, in other words the government. This principle was famously espoused by the French philosopher Montesquieu but also finds earlier expressions in the works of Aristotle, John Calvin, and John Locke. In administrative law, this distinction between the 'legality' and 'merits' of a decision is vitally important—though in some legal systems the distinction is blurred.

Tribunals are usually not part of the judiciary. In the likes of Australia and Hong Kong, they are part of the executive. So tribunals are not—indeed *cannot* be—courts because they are not part of the judicial branch (though, paradoxically, the President of the Australian Administrative Review Tribunal (ART) must be a Federal Court judge, so in Australia they are still managed by someone who is a member of the judicial branch). And because they are not part of the judicial branch, they are not prohibited from considering the merits of decisions. Inefficient, foolish, or hypocritical decisions can be and are changed by these tribunals. And the fact that tribunals can effectively *change* the decisions under challenge is another major difference from the work of a court reviewing government decisions for legality. Courts cannot and do not *change* unlawful government decisions. They can declare them to be void and of no legal effect, so that the original decision maker must remake the decision—this time lawfully—but the court will never substitute its own decision for the one that was declared to be unlawful. Why? Because that would violate the separation of powers rule by allowing the court to exercise power that was given by parliament (or the constitution) to the executive branch. Tribunals can change government decisions because tribunals are part of the executive, exercising some of the same powers as government decision makers. It can already be seen why it is fair to say that tribunals are somewhat like courts, but are not courts.

However, there is a problem. In the UK, tribunals used to be part of the executive branch, just like the legal systems mentioned above. In 1957 a committee of inquiry published an important document called the 'Franks Report' which asked whether tribunals should continue to be part of the 'machinery of administration' (i.e. part of the executive branch) or part of the 'machinery for adjudication' (i.e. more judicial in nature). The report answered that question by choosing the latter option: tribunals should be more judicial in nature because they adjudicate on disputes. A series of reforms was enacted. A further report called the 'Leggatt Report', published in 2001, went further. It led to reforms, including the Tribunals, Courts and Enforcement Act 2007, which essentially moved tribunals out of the executive branch and into the judicial branch—alongside courts. While there are some good reasons for doing that, how can these tribunals be distinguished from courts? Some leading experts in this field, such as Carol Harlow and Robert Thomas, argue that in the UK they essentially are courts: Harlow called them 'specialist courts with limited jurisdiction', while Thomas described them as 'specialist administrative courts'. But the question does remain why we, and they, continue to refer to 'courts *and tribunals*' in the UK rather than simply to 'courts'. Thus UK tribunals largely buck the trend here.

But they are not the only ones to do so. The US mostly has no equivalent to tribunals as they are found in the UK, Canada, Australia, India, or other common law jurisdictions. The US does have some specialist tribunals but the function of tribunals is largely played by review within executive agencies, which were discussed in Chapter 2. There are constitutional reasons for this, in particular the US's constitutional separation of powers between the legislative, executive, and judicial branches. Yet Australia, with its own strict constitutional separation of powers, has tribunals in the more traditional sense which are part of the executive but largely independent of government. And, just to throw a spanner in the works, some courts are called 'tribunals' (rather than being tribunals in the more traditional sense, like Hong Kong's Competition Tribunal), and some tribunals are not called 'tribunals' at all (like Hong Kong's Administrative Appeals Board).

This all seems like a bit of a mess. In many ways it is. There is a lot of uncertainty about what tribunals really are, how they are or should be different from other institutions like courts or internal government review procedures, and how they should fit into the broader system for challenging government decisions. Part of the reason for this is that tribunals have grown in a fairly sporadic and ad hoc way in a number of legal systems—this is true of such diverse jurisdictions as Hong Kong, Singapore, New Zealand, and Israel. Typically, individual tribunals have been created to deal with problems in particular areas, for example immigration, trade, or licensing. These can be highly specific, for example Hong Kong's Appeal Board (Lifts and Escalators Ordinance). But some larger, generalist tribunals have emerged in the common law jurisdictions. A major example is the Administrative Review Tribunal (ART) in Australia. While many of the appeals in the

ART are against migration decisions, it has the power to determine appeals against decisions made under more than 400 pieces of legislation in such diverse areas as social welfare, taxation, citizenship, and civil aviation. The ART's predecessor (the Administrative Appeals Tribunal) notably grew in size and generality of jurisdiction in 2015 when the Migration Review Tribunal, Refugee Review Tribunal, and Social Security Appeals Tribunal were merged with it. Other examples are the UK's First-tier Tribunal and Upper Tribunal which were created in 2008 as part of major reforms to the UK tribunal system. But many countries have no 'system' of tribunals at all, rather an assortment of ad hoc tribunals. Where the definition of a tribunal ends and another type of body begins is also open to dispute, as their work can blend into that of professional disciplinary panels, regulators, and other adjudicatory bodies.

One thing that all tribunals have in common, however, is that there must be some specific legal provision allowing a person to appeal to the tribunal. In common law systems, higher level courts often have an inherent jurisdiction to decide legal disputes which does not depend on specific legislative provisions. Tribunals do not have an inherent jurisdiction. Whereas a person can apply to a court for judicial review of almost any government decision, this is not true of appeals to tribunals. There must be a specific right of appeal to a tribunal created by legislation, and many government decisions will not have a right of appeal against them. This does not mean that those decisions are beyond challenge, it just means that any challenge will have to be made to a court for judicial review, and that can only be done on the basis that the decision is unlawful (see Chapter 4). In those cases, it simply will not be possible to seek merits review of the decision.

It is also worth stressing that, even though tribunals are under the spotlight to a lesser extent than courts both in the public consciousness and legal scholarship, they are a major coalface of administrative law, hearing thousands of appeals in important areas of people's lives. Some of the more common areas of decision making subject to tribunal jurisdiction are immigration, tax, housing, social welfare, licensing (in its many different forms), and urban planning. But there are also dozens of miscellaneous areas of decision making which can be appealed to tribunals, as diverse as environmental regulation, freedom of information, postal service disputes, transport registration, civil aviation, buildings regulation, employment, regulation of the professions, bankruptcy, insurance, financial services, charities regulation, education, telecommunications and broadcasting, compensation schemes, disability support, care support, mental health medicine and pharmaceutical regulation, scientific and technological regulation, health and safety, veterans' entitlements, citizenship, passports, security assessments…in other words, many and varied aspects of our lives. Tribunals are a major part of administrative law and administrative accountability.

Tribunals, even those outside the UK, do often operate like courts in significant ways. In some places, like Australia, tribunals must ensure they are not exercising judicial power because the Australian Constitution only permits judicial power to be exercised by courts, in accordance with the well-known decision of the High Court of Australia in *R v Kirby, ex parte Boilermakers' Society of Australia* [1956] HCA 10. Australian tribunals must still interpret and apply the law (though that is often true of many other government decision makers), but their main function is merits review, not review for legality. In other places, like Hong Kong, tribunals can evaluate the merits of decisions but also consider their legality, both because there is no constitutional prohibition on them considering legality and also because of the wording of the applicable legislation.

Tribunals often have powers similar to those of courts. For example, tribunals typically have rules about what evidence can be used. Many can administer oaths from oral witnesses with rules about examination and cross-examination of witnesses. There are rules about the order of proceedings, procedural time limits and the retrieval, use, and sharing of documents. Being dishonest to, or uncooperative with, a tribunal can constitute contempt with civil or criminal penalties, similar to contempt of court. In some tribunals it is permitted to have lawyers present, and often tribunal proceedings are open to the public, just like those of courts. There can also be similarities to courts in a more tangible sense, including the layout of rooms, the use of audio and transcription facilities, and the use of titles for tribunal members.

However, these similarities should not be carried too far, because tribunals are often less formal than courts and many have more flexibility in the control of their own proceedings than courts. For example, the rules of evidence are often less stringent than those found in courts and sometimes there are no formal rules of evidence at all. And here is a major difference between courts and tribunals. Courts in common law systems are bound by a doctrine of precedent, which means in general terms that courts are bound by the previous decisions of courts. Tribunals are not bound by the previous decisions of tribunals. The reason for this is that tribunals are assessing the merits of *individual* cases, thus it is not just about applying rules, but also applying other factors and considerations (like policies) that go into the making of executive decisions. This does not mean that tribunals are engaged in a decisional free-for-all. They will often pay attention to previously decided cases and policies and be inclined to adopt a consistent approach to like cases. But they are not bound by strict rules of precedent in the way that courts are bound. Tribunal decisions also tend to be less public or less easily accessible than court judgments. Tribunals can sometimes also, depending on the legal system and the individual tribunal concerned, engage in inquisitorial or mediative functions which are not carried out by courts in common law systems.

It is worth considering who sits on tribunals, making decisions on appeals. The answer to this partly depends on the legal system whose tribunals we are dealing with, and partly on the individual tribunal. In a country like the UK, where tribunals are paradoxically part of the judiciary, many tribunal members are in fact judges. Elsewhere, the position is more nuanced. Many tribunal members are not judges or even lawyers. Often they will be subject matter experts, such as medical doctors sitting on a hospital appeals tribunal or qualified engineers sitting on an urban planning tribunal. Sometimes they will not be subject matter experts but simply appointed on the basis of their professional skills and standing in the community. But for all our talk of the separation of powers, the lines are blurred when it is considered that the chairpersons of tribunals are often judges. As noted, this is even true of the President of the ART in Australia, who must be a currently serving judge of the Federal Court, even though Australia has a strict constitutional separation of powers. The President of the ART does not sit *as* a judge when deciding appeals in the ART, but there is no question that a 'judicial' mindset will be brought to bear on those appeals. Again, little is clear-cut when it comes to tribunals.

While the fact that UK tribunal members are often judges confounds the whole rationale for tribunals being distinct from courts, it does bring one notable advantage. Judges are independent of government. The concept of judicial independence is hugely important because it means that judges can rule on the legality of government decisions without fear or favour. Judges enjoy what is called 'security of tenure', meaning they are appointed indefinitely and vacate their office only in the event of death, incapacity, reaching retirement age, or engaging in misconduct. Tribunal members in the UK therefore enjoy the same independence from government that judges enjoy.

This is often less true elsewhere. In the likes of Hong Kong, tribunal members are appointed by government ministers who, directly or indirectly, are in charge of the very decision makers whose decisions the tribunal is reviewing. It is a similar story in

India where selection committees for the appointment of tribunal members are resourced or operated by government departments. In both places, tribunal members can be appointed on short tenure cycles or removed as a matter of executive discretion. This clearly gives rise to concerns that tribunal members are not sufficiently independent of government and fail to represent a genuine channel for challenging government decisions. More worryingly, tribunal members may be less critical of government decisions for fear of proving too much of a thorn in the side of the government and thus risk being removed from their position, or not reappointed at the next appointment round. Conflicts of interest are not unique to these jurisdictions. Australia's Administrative Appeals Tribunal was replaced by the ART in 2024 precisely because appointments to the former were regarded as highly politicized. In the US, the fact that the tribunal function is largely performed by executive agencies themselves—i.e. within government—raises obvious questions about institutional independence, but the US also has globally famous problems with politicized appointments even to its Supreme Court.

It can therefore be seen that tribunals, despite the conceptual and practical difficulties that follow from their straddling the executive-judicial function, are a major forum for challenging government decisions. Their relative lack of notoriety and coverage in academic scholarship should not detract from that fact.

Chapter 4
Judicial review

The rule of law demands that the law applies to everyone and that unlawful activities are prohibited no matter who commits them. That applies as much to a prime minister or executive agency head as it does to a low-ranking administrative officer in a government department. While senior government officials often have broader powers which can be far-reaching in some cases, there are *always* legal limits to what can be done. Judicial review is the process by which courts invalidate the acts and decisions of public bodies or officials that violate a constitutional code, legislation, or common law (judge-made) rule. Judicial review is therefore a crucial process for maintaining the rule of law because it ensures that no one—including people who make and enforce the law—is above the law.

Judicial review is one of the most important areas of administrative law. Often, it overshadows other areas to a greater extent than it should. Many administrative law courses at law schools are mostly, or only, about judicial review. Even though most administrative law challenges take place in other areas, like internal review and administrative tribunals, there is a good reason for placing so much emphasis on judicial review. That is because it is a back stop, a final guarantee that unlawful activities will be struck down by courts. Although the divide is not as stark as it may sound, we do not explore judicial review for violations of constitutional codes in this chapter because those would be classed as 'constitutional judicial review' rather than judicial review in a broader administrative law sense.

It must be remembered that administrative law does not encompass every legal challenge against a public sector body or official: suing them for breach of contract, negligence, or infringement of a property right will usually not raise administrative law questions. And those types of challenges will usually not use the discrete judicial review procedure that most jurisdictions have. Instead, judicial review is for challenging breaches of so-called public law duties. The classic example would be where a public authority which gets its powers from legislation (and most public authorities do) violates some provision in that legislation. This would be a breach of a public law duty and the court can put a stop to it. But, as we shall see in this chapter, a significant part of judicial review is not about breach of a statutory duty, but breach of a common law rule. In the UK, courts have built up their own common law rules about exercises of public power over the course of centuries, and these have in large measure been exported to, or imported by, common law jurisdictions around the world—from Australia, New Zealand, and Canada to Hong Kong, Singapore, and India. We will go through the main common law rules in the course of this chapter.

Courts award one or more 'remedies' to the person who has applied for judicial review, assuming that they are successful in their application. The main judicial review remedies include certiorari, mandamus, and prohibition. These names are no longer used in England where they are respectively called quashing orders, mandatory orders, and prohibiting orders, but they still retain their original names in places like Australia, Canada, and Hong Kong. *Certiorari* is an order of the court striking down, or invalidating, an unlawful act or decision. It makes the act or decision null and void as though it had never been made in the first place. *Mandamus* forces a decision maker to do something positive—for example, to hold a hearing or provide a statement of reasons for a decision. *Prohibition* prevents a decision maker from doing something unlawful in the future—for example, from proceeding with the deportation of an asylum seeker or the demolition of a building. Other remedies can also be granted—an order of *declaration* involves the court declaring legal rights and obligations, while a writ of *habeas corpus* allows a detained person to challenge the legality of their detention. However, generally speaking, *damages*, i.e. payment of money, cannot be obtained for breach of a public law duty. Damages tend only to be awarded by courts in a judicial review application where there is some specific statutory entitlement to money, for example legislation about compensation, in certain human rights contexts, or where there is also a private law aspect to the case like breach of contract or negligence. In the US, the main remedies are *injunction* and *declaratory judgment*.

This takes us to some key limitations to judicial review, notwithstanding its great importance. In administrative law we talk about challenging decisions, but as we touched on in Chapter 3 there are two different bases on which we can make those challenges. One is a challenge about the legality of a decision; the other is a challenge about the merits of a decision. Judicial review is *only* about challenging the legality of a decision, because courts only have the power to deal with legal issues (the US is something of an exception here). This is fundamentally because of the doctrine of the separation of powers, an idea developed by figures such as Aristotle, John Locke, and Montesquieu. Under the tripartite separation of powers, the power of the state is divided into three parts: legislative, executive, and judicial. Legislative power (the power to make law) is given to parliament. Executive power (the power to govern) is given to the government. Judicial power (the power to apply the law to decide legal disputes) is given to the courts. These distinctions are, in practice, not clean-cut. But what is important to understand is that courts only have the power to apply the *law* in judicial review procedure, not to substitute their own decision for the one that is being challenged. Whether the decision was good, bad, stupid, hypocritical, or inefficient is usually not a legal matter and the courts are not the place to entertain such complaints.

Merits review is quite different. This power is usually enjoyed by administrative tribunals, discussed in Chapter 3. Let us take an example. John has become unemployed and run into financial problems. He applies to his local housing authority for social housing. His application is rejected. John may have a statutory right to appeal to a tribunal. In all likelihood, the tribunal will be able to agree with the housing authority's decision or to disagree with it and *reverse* it. The tribunal can reverse the decision simply because it disagrees with it, perhaps because it was bad, stupid, hypocritical, or inefficient. In this example, the tribunal has just performed merits review, because it has assessed the merits of the original decision.

If John had chosen to apply for judicial review instead (though often he would be required to appeal to the tribunal first), the court could *not* conduct merits review because of the separation of powers rule. Questions about whether a decision is good or bad are usually not questions of law. Whereas a tribunal conducting merits review can reverse the original decision simply because it does not agree with it, a court conducting judicial review can *only* disturb the original decision if it has been found to be *unlawful*. While there are many ways in which the original housing decision could have been unlawful, this is a much narrower basis for challenging the decision than simply disagreeing with it. This turns out to be quite a major limitation on the role of judicial review. A court may think that the housing decision was a bad one and not the decision it would have made, but unless the court thinks it was unlawful, there is nothing it can do about it (again, the US is an exception here).

By final word of introduction, this also brings in another related distinction, which is between appeal and review. 'Appeal' usually refers to a situation where merits review is possible, such as where John appeals to the housing tribunal. But 'review' usually refers to a situation where review for legality is all that is possible, such as where John applies for judicial review. (The US does not recognize the same distinction between judicial review and statutory appeal.) For the avoidance of doubt, 'appeal' in this context is in general not referring to a situation where a person 'appeals' from a lower court to a higher court, as that raises different considerations.

Procedural issues

Judicial review usually involves a special procedure of the court which operates differently to procedures used in the likes of contract, negligence, and property litigation. As part of that special procedure, there are important rules and requirements which must be met. Two of particular importance are mentioned here: standing and the requirement for a sufficient public law element.

Judicial review often costs the taxpayer, because the public body that is taken to court must fork out considerable legal expenses. But the rule of law demands that public bodies are accountable in a court of law when they act unlawfully. So there must be a compromise. One aspect of that compromise is the rules on standing.

Standing is a requirement that the person applying for judicial review can show the court that they have a sufficient connection with the subject matter of the application. Sometimes this will be quite easy to establish. For example, a person who is refused public housing or a residence permit clearly has a sufficient connection with the alleged unlawful act to apply for judicial review. But this becomes less straightforward when a person, group, or association applies for judicial review on the basis that they 'represent' a specific cause. Should Greenpeace have standing to apply for judicial review of a government decision on air pollution? Should Greenpeace, Friends of the Earth, or the World Wildlife Fund have the strongest case for standing here? In fact, should they have any stronger a case for standing than any private individual, given that we all breathe this (polluted) air? Are they, or should they be, prioritized over a much smaller or more local environmental organization, noting that they will usually have much deeper pockets and better resources to challenge these decisions in court?

Courts across many common law jurisdictions such as the UK, Ireland, Australia, Canada, and Hong Kong have rules restricting standing on the basis of a sufficient connection. §702 of the US Administrative Procedure Act, which states that '[a] person suffering legal wrong because of agency action ... is entitled to judicial review thereof', is sometimes used by courts to head off public interest challenges. Some, like New Zealand, barely restrict standing, mainly because the jurisdiction is so small and the volume of cases so low. Others, like India, have not taken a strong line on this issue though this is clearly not because of the size of the jurisdiction. And there is an interesting tension here: if the rule of law tells us that public bodies must be accountable in a court of law for unlawful acts, why cannot anyone enforce that in court? The answer is one of pragmatism rather than principle—to allow that may well cost the taxpayer dearly.

Turning to a sufficient public law element: as already noted in this chapter, judicial review is a branch of public law. That concerns the public law duties of public bodies like government departments, public health authorities, licensing boards, planning authorities, and the police. It is not the appropriate legal channel for challenging the private law obligations of such bodies, such as those relating to contract, negligence, or property disputes. It is also not the appropriate legal channel for challenging non-public bodies, like individuals, private companies, and charities. But this can get very complex and, accordingly, messy.

In relation to the first issue, let us take the example of a public education authority. It is all very well to say that the public law duties of the education authority are enforceable through judicial review, whereas its private law obligations (contract, negligence, etc.) are enforceable through private law procedure. The problem is that cases may arise where public law and private law duties overlap and are intertwined. Employment disputes are typically private law in nature, but what if there are statutory regulations containing terms which are incorporated into the contracts of people employed by the education authority? What if the education authority exceeds the scope of its statutory powers when acting in the course of its contractual relationship with one of its employees? Is this a public law issue or a private law issue? Really it is both, but usually the person will have to choose between public law procedure (judicial review) and private law procedure. Selecting the wrong procedure can lead to the application failing which not only can result in wasted time and resources, but can also run into problems with time limits, remedies, and other procedural difficulties. This dual public law and private law scenario can also be found in other contexts, like public procurement, consumer law, and competition law.

In relation to the second issue, the divide between the public sector and the private sector is increasingly blurred. Governments began outsourcing many of their functions to private sector entities in the 1980s and that trend has largely continued. Private companies often deliver community health services, conduct welfare benefits assessments, run prisons, provide school meals, operate critical transport infrastructure, and provide security and facilities management services on behalf of the government. This has been taken to extremes—in Australia, private companies such as G4S and Serco have operated onshore and offshore government immigration detention centres. Does this change the nature of legal duties owed by the operator, or indeed by the government that engaged them? This is very far from being a theoretical question because the kinds of legal duties enforceable against public sector and private sector entities are generally quite different: for one thing, private sector individuals and entities usually cannot be pursued for breaching grounds of judicial review, nor are they usually on the hook for breaches of human rights. What about private companies set up and owned by national, state/devolved, or local governments to run or provide public services? These companies might be profitable, generating money for the government, or they might rack up huge debts. Are we in the realms of public law or private law here? For as long as there continue to be separate procedures and rules for public law and private law cases, this will continue to generate real practical difficulties.

A landmark English case which had varying effects throughout the common law world was *R v Panel on Take-overs and Mergers, ex parte Datafin* [1987] QB 815. Prior to *Datafin*, the availability of judicial review was primarily determined by whether the decision complained about was made in exercise of a statutory power, the underlying rationale being that only public bodies

3. A prison van operated by private company Serco: one of many examples at the interface of the public and private sectors.

enjoyed statutory powers. But the facts of *Datafin* exposed the flaws of this reasoning. An applicant company complained to the Panel on Take-overs and Mergers (a self-regulatory body) about the conduct of another company which it was alleged had breached the City Code on Take-overs and Mergers. The applicant company was dissatisfied with the Panel's decision and sought to challenge it by way of judicial review. Yet the Court of Appeal noted that the Panel was not acting in exercise of statutory powers when making its decision, which would normally make judicial review unavailable. However, there was no other legal route which could plausibly be used by the applicant company to challenge the legality of the Panel's actions. The court held that the Panel was performing public law functions; essentially that, although it was not strictly speaking a public body, it was acting like one. It was therefore subject to judicial review despite not exercising statutory powers: a major development in administrative law. The emphasis was shifted from the *source* of the body's powers to the *nature* of its powers when determining the availability of judicial review.

Following *Datafin*, a body that makes a decision that is akin to the exercise of a public function is amenable to judicial review. This was a welcome development in the law, moving away from a more rigid and outdated dichotomy between public bodies and private bodies, but ever since there has remained uncertainty and controversy on what exactly constitutes a 'public' function. It is worth noting that the *Datafin* approach has not been followed throughout the common law world—in Australia, for example, the availability of judicial review is determined by the identity of the party being sued (under section 75 of the Australian Constitution or section 39B of the Judiciary Act 1903) or the source of authority under which the decision was made (under the Administrative Decisions (Judicial Review) Act 1977), but in neither case by reference to the nature of the power exercised. This has led to cases which may have been decided differently had the *Datafin* approach been adopted.

An English case which wonderfully sums up just how difficult this public law/private law divide can be, how the whole framework can break down, and how practical can be its effects is *Crédit Suisse v Allerdale Borough Council* [1997] QB 306. Allerdale Borough Council was a local authority which set up a private company to circumvent borrowing restrictions incumbent upon it. The company took out a bank loan to finance a swimming pool and accommodation development. The Council acted as a guarantor for the loan. The money was spent and the company went into liquidation. The bank therefore sought to enforce the guarantee against the Council. The problem? The Council was in breach of its statutory duties in providing the guarantee in the first place. It is a fundamental principle of public law that a public body cannot do a thing that it has no legal power to do. If the Council had no legal power to guarantee the loan, then the guarantee was void. The bank therefore could not recover the debt of around £6 million. This is clearly not a satisfactory position and Australian administrative law professor Peter Cane wrote a very aptly titled article about the case called 'Do Banks Dare Lend to Local Authorities?' There are now protections against this kind of situation in the UK's Local Government (Contracts) Act 1997, but this was clearly a response to an existing problem and today there are still many other problems with this blurring of the public law and private law divide. This also continues to cause difficulties in other common law jurisdictions.

The grounds of judicial review

When a person applies for judicial review, they must demonstrate to the court that one or more 'grounds' of judicial review has been violated. This basically means stating what is legally wrong with the act or decision complained about. There are two potential targets here: (i) the process by which the decision was made, and (ii) the decision itself. It therefore follows that some of the grounds of review are geared more towards review of procedural issues while others are aimed at substantive issues. The grounds can come from three sources: constitutional instruments, legislation, and the common law.

Review under grounds contained in constitutional instruments is sometimes referred to as 'constitutional review'. The term 'constitutional instruments' is used here because it includes not only classic constitutional codes, like the US Constitution or the Australian Constitution, but also documents that have a quasi-constitutional status like the Canadian Charter of Rights and Freedoms or the Hong Kong Basic Law. The importance of this type of review can be underplayed, but this is really in the domain of constitutional law rather than administrative law (the two are closely related—there is often reference to 'constitutional and administrative law') so it is not given much coverage here. One of the most famous constitutional law cases in the common law world is the US case of *Marbury v Madison*, 5 US (1 Cranch) 137 (1803). The US Supreme Court decided that any congressional Act that violated the US Constitution had no legal effect because the Constitution was the highest law in the land. Another example from the US is *Engel v Vitale*, 370 US 421 (1962) where the Supreme Court decided that it was a violation of the First Amendment to the US Constitution—which states that Congress shall make no law respecting an establishment of religion or prohibiting the free exercise thereof—for New York schools to begin each day with a non-denominational prayer.

The second source of the grounds of judicial review is legislation. Sometimes legislation will set out the grounds of review in general terms. For example, in the US, the Administrative Procedure Act of 1946 sets out the grounds on which judicial review may lie against agency action. Similarly, the Administrative Decisions (Judicial Review) Act 1977 in Australia contains a list of grounds that was seen as an attempt to 'codify' the grounds of review (it didn't work). More often, including in Australia, individual statutes will provide grounds of review in particular areas of regulation. A good example is the Migration Act 1958 which governs, as the name suggests, immigration to Australia. Others include the Canadian Immigration and Refugee Protection Act 2001, the English Housing Act 2004, and the Irish Social Welfare Consolidation Act 2005. In fact, most judicial review applications relate to immigration, housing, social welfare, licensing, or planning.

The third source of grounds is the common law, in other words grounds that the courts have created and developed themselves. This chapter devotes most of its discussion to these grounds because (i) they help us to understand much of the logic of judicial review, and (ii) they apply to virtually *all* justiciable decisions taken by government and public bodies, and not just in particular areas like housing or immigration. It must be understood that there is no fixed or definitive list of common law grounds because they are still evolving and are derived from a vast number of cases rather than a published list. Often reference will be made to a famous statement by Lord Diplock in the English case of *Council of Civil Service Unions v Minister for the Civil Service* [1985] AC 374 that there are three grounds of judicial review, namely illegality, irrationality, and procedural impropriety. But it is unclear that Lord Diplock was trying to give a definitive account of the grounds—and plenty to suggest that he was not. Therefore, this chapter does not use that tripartite categorization. Instead, there can be said to be several more grounds; they do not always go by the same name within a country or between countries, but they cover broadly similar ground. It should be noted that although the grounds of review discussed in this chapter are characterized as common law grounds, they share a lot in common with the 'codified' grounds in the US Administrative Procedure Act of 1946 and the Australian Administrative Decisions (Judicial Review) Act 1977. In any event, these 'codified' grounds are interpreted and fleshed out by courts so the difference between them should not be exaggerated.

4. Lord Diplock was one of the most influential English judges of the 20th century and more broadly on judicial review in the common law world.

Before we explore these grounds, we need to briefly introduce the concept of discretion. In common parlance, 'discretion' is often used to express a person's power to make up their own mind or form their own assessment of matters. While that is true, in administrative law discretion is important because *all discretion is understood to have limits*. Yes, a government official or a public service employee may have 'discretion' when deciding whether to grant a visa, cancel a licence, reject a public housing application, and so on, but they cannot simply decide as they please. Their discretion must be exercised *lawfully*, and in particular *within the limits of their discretionary powers*. If they exceed the limits of their discretionary powers—whether by breaching a constitutional instrument, legislation, or common law ground—then judicial review is available to legally invalidate their action.

Excess of statutory powers and breach of statutory procedure

If legislation states that an official can decide A, B, or C, but the official purports to decide D, then that decision will be unlawful because the official has exceeded their statutory powers. An example could be where an immigration official tries to impose conditions on a person's residence permit, whereas the legislation might only give the official the power to award or decline to award the permit.

When courts are reviewing on this ground, they must necessarily interpret the legislation which governs the decision maker's powers and this can be a remarkably difficult exercise. Not only are vast areas of law highly complex, but legislation can also be confusing or poorly drafted, which adds to the problem. It might also be unclear what decision-making powers are implied by, or ancillary to, those that are clearly expressed in statutory provisions. Similarly, if the legislation sets up a decision-making procedure or imposes requirements like a duty to consult a body before making a decision, or a duty to give a licence applicant an oral hearing, what is the consequence of the decision maker failing to comply with these requirements? Does non-compliance void any decision that follows, or will the court have to decide whether parliament intended some other consequence (if any) to follow?

This ground is commonly invoked in judicial review applications, but of course it takes many different shapes and forms depending on the legislation which is alleged to have been breached.

Improper purposes, improper motives, and abuse of power

Sometimes a decision maker will make a decision that is technically within their powers. However, if that decision is taken for the wrong purposes, pursues improper motives, or involves any abuse of power, then it can be invalidated by a court in judicial review. This is closely related to a principle that emerged from the important English case of *Padfield v Minister for Agriculture, Fisheries and Food* [1968] AC 997 (HL), often called the '*Padfield* principle', which holds that decision makers must exercise statutory powers for the purposes and objects of the statute, and in particular, not for extraneous purposes.

A good example of this is where an immigration or security official makes an order to remove a person from the country. If the official has the legal power to deport a person (removal based on some kind of unlawful activity in the host country), but not to extradite them (removal because they are wanted for criminal proceedings in a third country), then they will have to ensure that the removal is in fact a deportation and not an extradition otherwise it will be unlawful. This situation has arisen in several countries. In the Australian case of *Schlieske v Minister for Immigration and Ethnic Affairs* (1988) 84 ALR 719, the government minister had signed an order deporting a man to what was then West Germany. However, the man was already wanted by West German authorities which had unsuccessfully sought extradition of him previously. The Australian government not only sought to deport the man to West Germany, but also to book his travel on a West German airline and take various other steps that made this look like an 'extradition in disguise'. The Federal Court of Australia ruled that the government could lawfully deport the man to West Germany, but ordered that additional steps such as delivering him into the hands of the West German authorities were prohibited. Deportation was a lawful purpose, whereas extradition would be an unlawful purpose, even though both involved sending the man from Australia to West Germany.

But much will depend on the impression formed by the judge about whether it is a bona fide deportation or an extradition in disguise. Two Hong Kong cases—*Re Lee Ching Ming* [1990] HKCFI 224 and *Meng Ching Hai v Attorney-General* [1991] 1 HKLR 535—failed to establish that what was really going on was an extradition in disguise, to Taiwan and Mainland China respectively. In a slightly older English case—*R v Governor of Brixton Prison, ex parte Soblen (No 2)* [1963] 2 QB 243—a similar challenge had also failed. But by no means has this ground been confined to the immigration and deportation/extradition context, having arisen in education, licensing, and policing contexts, to name a few others. It shows that even if a public authority's decision *looks* lawful on its face, courts are prepared to look behind the decision to see what was really motivating it. If that motive is unlawful, then the decision will also be unlawful. But much of this will come down to the evidence, because the motives for the decision might not be expressed in writing and broader facts may have to be examined by the court to establish the 'real' basis for the decision.

Irrelevant or impermissible considerations

The influential English judge, Lord Greene MR, said in the famous case of *Associated Provincial Picture Houses Ltd v Wednesbury Corporation* [1948] 1 KB 223 that:

> If in the statute conferring the discretion, there is to be found expressly or by implication matters which the authority exercising the discretion ought to have regard to, then in exercising the discretion it must have regard to those matters. Conversely, if the nature of the subject matter and the general interpretation of the

Act make it clear that certain matters would not be germane to the matter in question, the authority must disregard those irrelevant collateral matters.

Irrelevant or impermissible considerations can be closely related to improper purposes as a ground of review, but it is a ground in its own right. When a decision maker is making a decision, there are certain considerations they are not allowed to take into account; these are often called 'irrelevant considerations'. Conversely, there are considerations that decision makers *may* or *must* take into account; these are often called 'relevant considerations'. Taking an irrelevant consideration into account, or failing to take a relevant consideration into account, can give rise to the decision being invalidated by a court in a judicial review application.

What is relevant and irrelevant is mainly determined by reference to the legislation which confers the decision-making powers on the person or body in question. But that may involve questions of interpretation and implication. Section 5 of the UK's Planning Act 2008 requires government ministers, when producing National Policy Statements, to 'give reasons for the policy set out in the statement' and that the 'reasons must (in particular) include an explanation of how the policy set out in the statement takes account of Government policy relating to the mitigation of, and adaptation to, climate change'. In other words, the Planning Act 2008 makes government policy on climate change a relevant—indeed mandatory—consideration when exercising these powers.

This may sound quite straightforward but, as is often the case with administrative law (or perhaps the law generally), the reality can be more complex. In the Australian case of *Tickner v Chapman* (1995) 57 FCR 451, the Aboriginal and Torres Strait Islander Heritage Protection Act 1984 required the government minister to consider a 'report and any representations attached to the report'. The court held that the minister would have to personally read the 400 or so representations attached to the report and could not simply rely on summaries of them, though a government minister is no doubt under demanding time and capacity restraints. In addition, the minister—who was male—had not read two confidential representations which were sealed in an envelope. They had been written by indigenous Ngarrindjerri women and purported to contain secret folklore knowledge which, according to custom, should not be read by men. Accordingly, a female official read those representations and assured the male minister that they contained nothing that materially changed the overall context of the decision. The court ruled that the male minister must still personally read those representations even if it conflicted with 'a system of beliefs and traditions originating in times when such external elements [as the requirements of administrative law] were entirely absent'. Given the political, social, and cultural sensitivities of indigenous relations in Australia, that is a controversial finding, but one which illustrates well how something as seemingly technical and esoteric as the requirements of relevant considerations in administrative law can run into much broader difficulties.

Unlawful delegation, divestiture, and relinquishment

Most decision-making powers derive their legal authority from legislation. If the legislation specifies that Official X has the power to make a decision, Official X cannot delegate that decision-making power to Official Y. To do so would undermine the intention of parliament that it is Official X who makes the decision. This is encapsulated in a Latin phrase that is often used to describe this rule, *delegatus non potest delegare*—literally meaning 'a person who has had power delegated to them cannot further delegate that power'.

This sounds good in theory. But legislation often vests decision-making powers in officials who simply do not have the time or capacity to make all of those decisions personally—government ministers for large, complex departments, such as home affairs, immigration, transport, and the like. In practice, those ministers often delegate decision-making powers to officials in their department. This has been tolerated in the UK on the basis of the 'Carltona principle'—drawn from the eponymous English case of *Carltona Ltd v Commissioner of Works* [1943] 2 All ER 560—which says that a departmental official can exercise power on behalf of the government minister. The principle has been justified not only on the basis of practicalities (how can a busy minister personally read hundreds if not thousands of pages of materials each day when making decisions that are legally taken in their name?), but because the minister in whose name the decision is made is constitutionally accountable to parliament—noting that government ministers are by convention drawn from parliament.

The *Carltona* principle does not apply to other kinds of decision makers beyond those in government departments, where the general rule against delegation applies (unless, of course, the legislation expressly or impliedly permits delegation). The court will nevertheless still look to the legislation to see whether the government minister should consider the matter personally rather than for a civil servant to consider it on their behalf. The UK Supreme Court underlined this principle in *R v Adams* [2020] UKSC 19. Irish republican politician Gerry Adams was detained in 1973 under the Detention of Terrorists (Northern Ireland) Order 1972. It later transpired, under the UK rule that government documents be made publicly available after 30 years, that the minister had not considered the matter personally. The court held that on a proper interpretation of the Order the minister should have considered the matter personally and, having failed to do so, the detention and related convictions of Adams were unlawful. Government ministers, and other decision makers, therefore have to take great care when considering whether to delegate decision-making powers to others. More routine decisions are more likely to be amenable to lawful delegation, whereas more high-level decisions are less likely to be lawfully delegated; though there is no one-size-fits-all rule here.

In addition, the constitutional justification for the *Carltona* principle is weaker or absent in some other legal systems where such delegation does take place in practice. For example, in Hong Kong, government ministers are not drawn from the territory's parliament, the Legislative Council, and while there are provisions in the territory's Basic Law (its 'mini-constitution') that there is some executive accountability to the Legislative Council, it is a far weaker form of accountability than UK government ministers have to the UK Parliament. In general, this ground is an area where there is a fair amount of divergence among common law countries. In India, the rule against delegation is not as strictly applied (*Sahni Silk Mills (P) Ltd v ESI Corp* (1994) 5 SCC 346), whereas in Canada it is more strictly applied (*Brant Dairy Co Ltd v Milk Commission of Ontario* [1973] SCR 131).

Fettering of discretion

A fetter is literally a chain or manacle which restricts movement. A fetter in administrative law is metaphorically the same thing—something that restricts the decision maker's area of discretionary 'movement'. If parliament enacts legislation which confers decision-making powers on a decision maker, it is not open to the decision maker to do anything that restricts those decision-making powers. For example, if the legislation states that the decision maker can decide A, B, or C, but the decision maker resolves never to decide C, then this is unlawful fettering of discretion. Why? Because Parliament intended that C would sometimes be decided, and it is contrary to parliamentary intention for the decision maker to resolve never to decide C.

Quite often this is seen in relation to the adoption of policies by government departments. Policies can help decision makers to improve the quality and consistency of their decisions, but they must be careful that a policy is not a fetter on their discretion. An example comes from the English case of *R v Secretary of State for the Home Department, ex parte Venables* [1998] AC 407. The government minister adopted a policy which precluded him and the Parole Board from having any regard to the circumstances and welfare of child murderers for a period of 12 years' detention. This was held by the House of Lords to be an unlawful fetter on the minister's discretion and, as the judge Lord Browne-Wilkinson explained in the case, both the policy and any decisions taken under it were unlawful.

But this does not mean that policies can never state that—to use the above example—C would not *normally* be decided. There might be good reasons for adopting such a policy. However, in order for this to remain lawful, it would have to be evident that the decision maker is still genuinely prepared to make an exception to their policy and to decide C. If exceptions are never made, the courts are likely to take a dim view of the authenticity of the decision maker's position and may void the policy and any decisions taken under it. The case of *R v Warwickshire County Council, ex parte Collymore* [1995] ELR 217 provides a good example of this. A local education authority adopted a policy under which there would be no provision for new discretionary awards due to the financial position of the authority (and with the effective bankruptcy of Birmingham City Council in 2023, this is as pertinent a consideration as ever). On paper there were exceptions. But, apart from in two cases where the authority honoured existing commitments, the authority rejected every appeal in over 300 applications made over a three-year period. The judge ruled that it was 'impossible to escape the conclusion that in practice the policy has been implemented far too rigidly' and that the 'application was not properly considered'. Whereas decision makers cannot exceed the limits of their discretionary authority, fettering of discretion is the other side of this coin in that decision makers must be prepared to exercise the full extent of their discretionary authority.

Factual and legal errors

Administrative lawyers sometimes speak of 'errors of fact' and 'errors of law'. These can be quite difficult to distinguish from each other, but at their core, the decision maker has made a decision based on some kind of error. Here is an example. A person applies to a tax authority for commercial property tax relief for a property at 5 Melbourne Court. The tax authority believes that 5 Melbourne Court is a residential property and on that basis refuses the application. In fact, the property is a coffee shop and would qualify for the tax relief. The tax authority has made a factual error (which subsequently becomes a legal error).

Here is a slightly different example. A person applies to the tax authority for commercial property tax relief for a property at 110 Pacific Drive. The property at that address is a privately run residential care home. The tax authority classifies this as a residential property and therefore refuses the application. But the applicant applies to a court for judicial review which confirms that a privately run residential care home is a 'commercial property' and would therefore qualify for the tax relief. This is not a factual error, but it is a legal error on the part of the tax authority because it has misinterpreted the legal meaning of 'commercial property'.

In these situations, the tax authority can be said to have done something it was not legally entitled to do. Error of law is one of the most complex aspects of judicial review and this is not the place for an in-depth discussion of it. Additionally, the concept of error of law is more firmly rooted in the law of judicial review of some countries, such as Australia, where a highly troublesome distinction between 'jurisdictional errors' and 'non-jurisdictional errors'—a distinction that was effectively abolished in the UK, Ireland, New Zealand, and South Africa—still persists. The law in this area is the stuff of nightmares and it is mentioned here for one purpose only: to draw attention to ouster clauses.

Ouster clauses, also known as privative clauses, are provisions in legislation which purport to limit or exclude the possibility of judicial review. A well-known example of an ouster clause from the UK was section 4(4) of the Foreign Compensation Act 1950 which related to the Foreign Compensation Commission, a body which determined payments for compensation following the Suez Crisis: 'The determination by the Commission of any application made to them under this Act shall not be called in question in any court of law.' This clause was held by the House of Lords in *Anisminic v Foreign Compensation Commission* [1969] 2 AC 147 not to oust the jurisdiction of the courts to judicially review the Commission where it exceeded its legal powers by making an error of law.

A more recent example from the UK is section 67(8) of the Regulation of Investigatory Powers Act 2000 which dealt with the powers of the Investigatory Powers Tribunal: 'Except to such extent as the Secretary of State may by order otherwise provide, determinations, awards, orders and other decisions of the Tribunal (including decisions as to whether they have jurisdiction) shall not be subject to appeal or be liable to be questioned in any court.' This clause was likewise held by the UK Supreme Court in *R (on the application of Privacy International) v Investigatory Powers Tribunal* [2019] UKSC 22 not to oust the courts' jurisdiction to judicially review the Tribunal.

A similar approach is found in other legal systems. An example from Hong Kong is section 64(3) of the Interpretation and General Clauses Ordinance which dealt with the jurisdiction of the chief executive in council: 'no proceedings by way of mandamus, certiorari, prohibition, injunction or other order shall be taken against the Chief Executive in Council in respect of any such appeal or objection to the Chief Executive in Council or any proceedings connected therewith.' Similarly, this clause was held in *Gurung Bhakta Bahadur v Director of Immigration* [2001] 3

HKLRD 225 not to oust the courts' jurisdiction to judicially review the Chief Executive in Council.

Why do these ouster clauses not protect such bodies from judicial review, even when parliament has used clear language to that effect? The answer is that, if ouster clauses *did* exclude the possibility of judicial review, parliament would be simultaneously conferring limited powers on decision makers but then denying the very means (judicial review) by which any excess of those powers could be challenged. This would weaken the rule of law because decision makers would be unable to be challenged in a court of law when acting unlawfully. Ouster of jurisdiction to judicially review would be to hand the decision maker discretionary carte blanche.

But in Australia, this is only true where the decision maker does something that is classed as a 'jurisdictional error'. By contrast, non-jurisdictional errors can sometimes be saved from judicial review. This is because section 75(v) of the Australian Constitution guarantees an 'entrenched minimum provision of judicial review' in relation to jurisdictional matters, as decided by the High Court in *Plaintiff S157/2002 v Commonwealth* (2003) 211 CLR 476. Similarly, the Supreme Court of Canada held in *Crevier v Attorney General (Québec)* [1981] 2 SCR 220 that where a provincial legislature tried to insulate one of its statutory tribunals from judicial review, including on jurisdictional grounds, that would be unconstitutional as incompatible with section 96 of the Constitution Act 1867. So too is the Indian Constitution relevant in that country's treatment of this area of law, which also prevents ouster clauses from excluding judicial review of certain types of decisions. If ouster clauses tell us one thing, it is that the law cannot be gleaned simply from a plain reading of the words of legislation—what really matters is what the courts say those words mean. Even in the US, where §701(a)(1) of the Administrative Procedure Act permits statutes to preclude judicial review, what this means in practice is still subject to judicial interpretation.

Finally, it should be noted in this section that not all ouster clauses are the same in form and extent. Some purport to comprehensively exclude judicial review, and those will tend to run into the strongest judicial resistance. However, some will try to limit rather than exclude the availability of judicial review, such as on the range of grounds or subject matter on which review is permitted, or to impose time limits after which review is not available. These are more likely to be tolerated by courts and recognized as lawful, but it will depend on the extent to which this limited ouster undercuts the courts' jurisdiction to review for excess of power, particularly where jurisdictional errors are at issue.

Breach of legitimate expectations

There is considerable variation across the common law jurisdictions in treatment of this ground. For example, while legitimate expectations are an accepted part of English law, they have largely been rejected in Australian law.

Legitimate expectations relate to a statement, practice, or context giving rise to an expectation that something will be done or given. They fall into two categories. Procedural expectations, as the name suggests, are about something a person expects to receive procedurally—that could be a meeting with an official or an oral hearing before a tribunal. Substantive expectations are about something a person expects to receive substantively—for example, a licence, planning permission, or public housing. Procedural expectations are more likely to be protected by courts than substantive expectations, for the reason that public authorities have the right to change their minds on substantive issues and to have regard to changing priorities, resource, and policy considerations. By contrast, individuals are still entitled to be treated fairly as a matter of procedure even where a public authority changes its substantive policies.

An excellent, though unusual, example which illustrates protection of a legitimate expectation is the English case of *R v North and East Devon Health Authority, ex parte Coughlan* [2001] QB 213. Mrs Coughlan was severely disabled. She and seven others had been moved from a public hospital to a public nursing home. In an effort to persuade Mrs Coughlan and the other patients to make this move, the local health authority assured them that the nursing home would be their 'home for life'. Around five years later, the health authority sought to close the nursing home. Mrs Coughlan applied to the court for judicial review on the basis that the specific promise of a home for life constituted a legitimate expectation that the authority would not seek to close the nursing home a few years later. She was successful and the decision to close the nursing home was voided by the court. It should be emphasized that this was an unusual decision because courts are usually quite reluctant to protect substantive expectations, such as where someone lives. In addition, a promise of this nature would not have been protected in the same way in a jurisdiction like Australia—at least under the heading of legitimate expectations—but it gives a good illustration of what legitimate expectations are all about.

As mentioned earlier, there is significant overlap between the grounds of judicial review, and different legal systems sometimes tackle the same issue under different grounds. Australia would likely treat the above scenario as a procedural fairness issue; so would Canada and India. Legitimate expectations and procedural fairness are tied together as issues in South Africa. But in the UK, Ireland, and New Zealand, legitimate expectations are often treated as more of a standalone ground, albeit that it again tends to feature more in a procedural than substantive context.

Unreasonableness and irrationality

This is one of the most controversial grounds of judicial review, for it takes judges dangerously close to merits review which is prohibited by the constitutional separation of powers. Judges are supposed to be confined to assessing the legality of a decision, not whether it is good or bad, but this ground involves a judge asking whether a decision is 'so unreasonable that no reasonable decision maker could have arrived at it'. This circular formulation, and variations on it, derived from a famous statement of Lord Greene MR in the English case of *Associated Provincial Picture Houses Ltd v Wednesbury Corporation* [1948] 1 KB 223, so famous that the test is often referred to as '*Wednesbury* unreasonableness'. The facts of the case were less remarkable than its legacy for administrative law Wednesbury Corporation, which was a local authority, imposed on the proprietors of a cinema a licence condition stipulating that, on Sundays, 'no children under the age of fifteen years shall be admitted to any entertainment, whether accompanied by an adult or not'. The court reasoned that it was technically within the statutory powers of the local authority to impose this condition. However, Lord Greene added in what is now regarded as a classic statement of the law that 'although the local authority have kept within the four corners of the matters which they ought to consider, they have nevertheless come to a conclusion so unreasonable that no reasonable authority could ever have come to it' (*sic*). The court held that the local authority did not breach this standard, so it is odd that Lord Greene's statement has accumulated such weight of authority. Yet it remains, almost 80 years later, the starting point for any discussion of this ground of review.

The justification for unreasonableness as a ground of review is that parliament—which usually is the source of the legal authority for the decision maker to make a decision—cannot possibly have intended that a decision would be made which is 'so outrageous in its defiance of logic or of accepted moral standards', as put by Lord Diplock in the case of *Council of Civil Service Unions v*

5. The former Gaumont Cinema in Wednesbury, West Midlands, UK; the unlikely subject of one of the most well-known rules of judicial review in the common law world.

Minister for the Civil Service [1985] AC 374. However, judges have traditionally set the bar at a high level under this ground so that it has been comparatively difficult to plead it successfully in court. A judge in an early 20th-century case gave the example of a teacher dismissed because she had red hair. But there are difficulties in quantifying exactly how the success of this ground compares to that of others due to various factors ranging from the quirks of law reporting to overlap with grounds pleaded in constitutional or human rights contexts, such as European Convention of Human Rights claims made under the UK's Human Rights Act 1998.

One issue with this ground is that the bar seems to have been lowered in some cases. An entertaining example from Hong Kong is the case of *Zestra Asia Ltd v Commissioner for Transport* [2007] 4 HKLRD 722. The Commissioner for Transport had the statutory power to reject a Personalized Vehicle Registration Mark

(PVRM) (basically a private licence plate) deemed offensive to good taste and decency. Zestra had applied for a PVRM in the name of 'Zestra', which was rejected. Zestra manufactured female sexual arousal products, but the evidence for the name being deemed to be offensive was lacking. The Commissioner had consulted three bodies whose responses it deemed to support its conclusion that 'Zestra' was offensive. It consulted the police, who did not respond; the Home Affairs Bureau, who replied with a mere description of Zestra's products; and the Official Languages Division, which ironically referred to Zestra's products as 'tropical' rather than 'topical'. None of the responses could be said to support the Commissioner's finding that the 'Zestra' PVRM would be considered offensive. Similarly, the Commissioner had said that the local Chinese population was sexually conservative and would be offended by the appearance of 'Zestra' on a licence plate, but offered no evidence in support of this.

The court ruled that the Commissioner's decision was *Wednesbury* unreasonable. It might indeed be unreasonable in a generic sense, but in a legal sense? The traditionally high threshold for making out this ground appeared to have been significantly lowered. As this was only the decision of a lower court, its long-standing effect remains to be seen. It is a good illustration, however, of the kinds of situations where what is *legally* unreasonable is very much up for debate. It also shows that even if a decision maker does something which is technically within the four corners of their powers, if a court regards it to be legally unreasonable or irrational, then it can invalidate the decision. If readers are wondering how this is *not* a court evaluating the merits of the decision—which we know they are prohibited from doing under the constitutional separation of powers—that is a very good question. And one to which there is no fully convincing answer, other than to say that the courts would never admit to looking at the merits and that judges have generally imposed a high threshold for success under this ground.

In the US, the bar for unreasonableness review is lower than in jurisdictions like Australia and Hong Kong. §706(2)(A) of the Administrative Procedure Act (and corresponding provisions in state law) provides for the statutory ground 'arbitrary, capricious, an abuse of discretion, or otherwise not in accordance with law'. This is usually referred to as the 'arbitrary and capricious' or 'abuse of discretion' standard. Cases like *Citizens to Preserve Overton Park v Volpe*, 401 US 402 (1971) established the extent to which courts can conduct unreasonableness review in the US, with cases such as *Motor Vehicle Manufacturers Association v State Farm Mutual Automobile Insurance Co*, 463 US 29 (1983) and *Salameda v Immigration and Naturalization Service*, 70 F.3d 447 (7th Cir. 1995) showing the extent to which courts may impose quite demanding reasoned decision-making obligations on agencies. It is also worth noting that the unreasonableness standard has been more flexibly applied in modern times in jurisdictions such as England, for example in the human rights context.

Proportionality

When discretion is being exercised, there will often be more than one possible decision that can be made. Some decisions would clearly be unlawful because they are beyond the scope of the body's decision-making authority. But there may be more than one *lawful* decision that can be made. Traditionally, the courts have left it to the decision maker to choose which *lawful* decision to make because executive decision makers bear political/democratic responsibility for policy choices and, under the constitutional separation of powers, should enjoy a degree of executive discretion. Decision makers will also tend to have greater substantive expertise in the relevant area of decision making than the court. However, if the proportionality ground applies, the range of *lawful* decisions which can be made by the decision maker becomes more restrictive. Though the exact construction of proportionality tests varies between legal systems, these will generally involve the court investigating whether the decision pursued a legitimate aim, whether it was rationally connected to that aim, whether it was no more than necessary to achieve that aim, and whether it struck a fair balance between individual rights and the public interest. The overarching justification for the proportionality test is that rights should be impacted as narrowly as possible by decisions, and so the test is designed to have a moderating influence on public decision making.

Proportionality does find some historical traction in the common law protection of fundamental rights. For example, in the English case of *R v Barnsley Metropolitan Borough Council, ex parte Hook* [1976] 1 WLR 1052, a market trader was seen by council employees to urinate in a side street near the market when the public toilets were closed. The matter was taken up through the council which ultimately terminated the trader's licence to operate a stall in the market. The English Court of Appeal held that the punishment was too severe—effectively too disproportionate to the act complained of—and quashed it as such. But proportionality has not developed into an independent common law ground of review. Lord Diplock said in *Council of Civil Service Unions v Minister for the Civil Service* [1985] AC 374 that proportionality might in the future be adopted as a ground of judicial review, but generally speaking it has not been so adopted.

Proportionality does continue to feature in judicial review applications in the UK involving the European Convention on Human Rights and what is left of European Union law, but unreasonableness has been regarded as a more appropriate general ground of review than proportionality. Why? Because if unreasonableness takes the courts dangerously close to merits review, then proportionality may do so to an even greater extent, further eroding the range of decisions that can lawfully be made by the decision maker. It must be remembered that courts are only supposed to assess whether a decision is lawful, not whether it is good or bad or whether some other decision might have been more appropriate. However, a key part of proportionality analysis is to ask whether some more proportionate decision might have been made by the decision maker. It is difficult for the court to ask that question without starting to weigh up different possible decisions which involve policy considerations the likes of which are for the executive—not the judiciary—to appraise.

Courts in more recent times do sometimes adopt a proportionality analysis as part of their reasoning, and the UK Supreme Court's discussion in the case of *Keyu v Secretary of State for Foreign and Commonwealth Affairs* [2015] UKSC 69 shows how proportionality can blend into irrationality. But the court was unwilling in that case to make the leap from irrationality to proportionality 'because it would involve the court considering the merits of the decision at issue' which 'would appear to have potentially profound and far-reaching consequences'. Proportionality thus continues not to stand on its own two feet as a common law ground of review. This is even truer in Australia, with its more rigid separation of powers thanks to the Australian Constitution; general human rights legislation features only in the state of Victoria and the Australian Capital Territory. The Canadian, Irish, and New Zealand situations are not entirely dissimilar to the UK's, inasmuch as reasonableness tends to be used as the standard of review, with proportionality largely reserved for human rights challenges. India has largely reserved proportionality for constitutional review, as has Hong Kong. It is therefore insightful that in none of these jurisdictions is proportionality freely available as a general ground of review, even among systems that have varying forms of constitutional and human rights codes. Of course, that can change, but there is no sign that this development is imminent.

Procedural fairness and the rules of natural justice

A great part of judicial review is concerned with issues of procedure and one of the most substantial procedural aspects relates to so-called procedural fairness and the rules of natural justice. This has a long history, far preceding the advent of modern judicial review and even the modern English legal system (which is the main historical source of most of the common law world's systems of judicial review). Foundational concepts of equity and justice are found in the laws of Ancient Greece, India, and biblical sources. But the concept took root in the modern common law world in cases from around the 15th century onwards. For example, in the English *Bagg's Case* (1615) 11 Co Rep 93, the chief burgess of Plymouth was reinstated to his position having been removed from it without being given notice or a hearing. Typically the concept of procedural fairness was found in a judicial setting where ideas of fair play were developed. This occurred not just in England but elsewhere; in Scotland, for example, a number of 18th-century cases refer to concepts such as 'the eternal principles of justice', 'the principles of fair justice between man and man', and 'equal justice between the parties'.

Yet some distinct attributes to this fuzzy notion of procedural fairness emerged. One of the most important is the right to be heard. In a court, this means that a judge should not be making judgment in a case without hearing what both parties have to say—that may seem obvious but it was not always the case, and it is still not the case in various authoritarian states in the modern world. But the idea, and indeed the rule, that a person should be given a fair hearing bled over into other areas that did not involve courts or judges. A government department exercising appellate functions should 'fairly listen to both sides' (*Board of Education v Rice* [1911] AC 179). So should arbitrators (*Re Brook* (1864) 143 ER 1184), clubs exercising disciplinary functions (*Innes v Wylie* (1844) 1 Car & Kir 257), and local police authorities that could discipline police officers (*Ridge v Baldwin* [1964] AC 40). There are several aspects to what a fair hearing can require. These range from giving a party sufficient notice of a case or charge against them, or giving them sufficient information to state a meaningful case or defence (effectively a duty of disclosure); to whether an oral hearing should be given and whether a legal representative can be brought to and/or participate in such a hearing. These requirements will be determined by what is provided in the governing legislation and common law requirements; sometimes a constitutional provision can also require a hearing to be conducted, such as in terms of the due process clause in the Fifth and Fourteenth Amendments to the US Constitution.

There are other aspects to procedural fairness such as whether reasons should be given for a decision. It is easy to see why being given reasons for the refusal of a public housing application or planning application, for example, can enable a person to understand whether the refusal was lawful, fair, and free from error. If a person has a right to appeal against that refusal, it is also fairer if they are supplied with reasons for the refusal so that they are able to properly formulate their arguments at the appeal stage. In several common law jurisdictions, including England, Australia, and Hong Kong, there is no automatic common law right to receive reasons for a decision (or no corresponding duty on the decision maker to provide them). But the courts have held that, if fairness requires that reasons are given, then they must be given. That might occur in situations of significant factual or legal complexity, where a negative decision could cause significant detriment to the person affected or where the decision seems unusual or out of line with previous decisions. In some situations, this question is moot because legislation has provided that reasons must be given by certain decision makers. For example, in Australia, individuals subject to decisions which are liable to judicial review under the Administrative Decisions (Judicial Review) Act 1977 or to tribunal review under the Administrative Review Tribunal Act 2024 have a statutory right to require reasons to be given.

Another important strand to procedural fairness is the rule against bias. This was again originally seen in relation to judges but now applies to most decision makers including in administrative tribunals, government departments, sporting clubs, and voluntary associations. The rule is, at its core, very simple: the decision maker must be sufficiently impartial otherwise their decision stands to be voided by a court. But as usual the devil is in the detail. Bias falls into two categories—actual bias and apparent bias. Actual bias is difficult to prove in a court because it essentially requires proof of a state of mind. Most successful cases on bias are therefore about apparent bias—in those an applicant is instead trying to prove that the decision maker *appears* to be biased or that there is a significant enough risk that they are biased. As famously put by Lord Hewart in the English case of *R v Sussex Justices, ex parte McCarthy* [1924] 1 KB 256, '[j]ustice must not only be done, but must also be seen to be done'. Appearances really do matter under this head of review.

Sometimes the potential for bias is so significant that it leads to 'automatic disqualification', i.e. the decision maker cannot participate in the decision at all. This was illustrated in the unusual English case of *R v Bow Street Stipendiary Magistrate, ex parte Pinochet (No 2)* [2000] 1 AC 119. The House of Lords voided its own previous decision because one of the judges who had participated in the case, Lord Hoffmann, had links with Amnesty International which had long campaigned for legal accountability for the alleged crimes against humanity of former President of Chile, Augusto Pinochet. The case had concerned the question of whether Pinochet enjoyed immunity from extradition to Spain while in London for medical treatment; the newly constituted House of Lords panel ruled that Lord Hoffmann's connections with Amnesty International were significant enough to disqualify him from hearing the case, even though there was no suggestion that Lord Hoffmann was in fact biased.

But it does not always work out this way. In a rather odd case in Hong Kong, *Secretary for Justice v Li Chau Wing* [2004] HKCFI 1048, a lorry driver had been charged with road traffic offences after an accident which killed 20 bus passengers. The trial judge had to decide between a lesser and a more serious charge, but had been overheard a few days earlier at a conference commenting that he was dealing with a case involving a bus accident and believed the lesser charge was of little efficacy. Not only did the defence object to the judge's participation in the trial, so did the prosecution. To no avail, for the judge refused to step down and an urgent application for judicial review was rejected on the basis that there could be no real perception of bias on the trial judge's part and that his comments were merely 'jurisprudential' and 'philosophical'.

In the US, these matters are regarded as aspects of due process and are protected by the Fifth Amendment (at the federal level) and the Fourteenth Amendment (at the state and local level) to the US Constitution. There are also specific provisions on procedural fairness in the Administrative Procedure Act. For example, §555(b) provides that a person compelled to appear in person before an agency or representative thereof is entitled to be accompanied, represented, and advised by counsel or, if permitted by the agency, by another qualified representative. Procedural fairness provisions are also found in state legislation, such as §303 of New York's State Administrative Procedure Act which provides that hearings shall be conducted in an impartial manner, and §2.2-4024.1 of Virginia's Administrative Process Act which provides that a presiding officer or hearing officer is subject to disqualification for any factor that would cause a reasonable person to question their impartiality including bias, prejudice, financial interest, or *ex parte* communications.

Chapter 5
From ombudsmen to public inquiries: Other administrative law controls

There is a vast, diverse range of other administrative law controls beyond the coalfaces of internal review, administrative tribunals, and judicial review. These are so extensive, in fact, that they cannot be comprehensively detailed across the various countries in the common law world and beyond. However, an attempt is made in this chapter to give as broad an overview as possible of other types of administrative law controls, ranging from ombudsmen and anti-corruption bodies to public auditors and public inquiries.

Ombudsmen

Most readers with prior experience of using an ombudsman service will probably have encountered it in a private sector context. Some of these services are established by legislation but provide a dispute resolution service or complaints mechanism against private sector entities. For example, the UK's Financial Ombudsman Service handles complaints against financial services providers, while the Pensions Ombudsman handles complaints against pensions trustees and managers. Others are voluntary schemes operated by independent organizations, such as the UK's Furniture & Home Improvement Ombudsman which handles complaints against furniture retailers.

Ombudsmen perform a slightly different role in an administrative law context. The ombudsman—which takes its name from the eponymous Swedish institution—is an official or agency that monitors the activities of government for 'maladministration'. Maladministration, as the name suggests, is poor administrative practice and although unlawful activities would usually fall within its definition, it clearly goes far beyond the realms of illegality. Most of us have encountered maladministration in one form or another when dealing with public bodies, from inconsistent advice, incompetence and inefficiency to poor staff attitude, unreasonably long call waiting times, and unresponsive email accounts. It is obvious why these are undesirable traits for a public body to have—it makes them less responsive, less accountable, and reduces the value for money of taxes invested in them. In short, it lowers the standards of public service delivery.

We can therefore complain to an ombudsman in a much wider range of circumstances than those in which we could apply to a court for judicial review. There are also other reasons favouring the submission of an ombudsman complaint: it is usually quick, easy to understand, and low cost or even free of charge. In fact, it is provided in Principle 15 of the European Commission for Democracy through Law's *Venice Principles* that 'any individual or legal person, including NGOs, shall have the right to free, unhindered and free of charge access to the Ombudsman, and to file a complaint'. The accessibility of the ombudsman system, in contrast to judicial review in particular, is one of its great strengths. In many countries, all that is required is for a form to be completed, an email to be sent, or a phone call to be made. The ombudsman may come back to the complainant to request more information, but that is generally the end of the complainant's involvement in the process. In most cases the use of an ombudsman will be a low-risk, or risk-free, option for complaining about maladministration in a public body.

In contrast to court proceedings, where the litigant must proactively make the arguments, lead the evidence, and present the case, the ball is very much in the ombudsman's court once the complaint is submitted. The ombudsman also has great flexibility in how their investigations are conducted. They usually take place in private and are conducted informally. With hearings not usually being held, there is little need for rules of procedure, evidence, and cross-examination. The ombudsman does not sit like a judge or even a tribunal member 'deciding' what will happen in a dispute. Instead, their investigation is geared towards getting to the bottom of what has actually happened in a particular case; finding out the 'truth' of the matter. The ombudsman will use the complaint to guide their own investigations including communications with the official or department that is the subject of the complaint. To achieve that goal, the ombudsman usually has statutory powers to obtain evidence (in the loose sense of the word) from the relevant government department, interview officials, and inspect documents and records. All of this will be used by the ombudsman to make a finding and issue a report.

The question then becomes what the ombudsman can do about any maladministration that has been uncovered, and the answer may be surprising: very little. The ombudsman cannot award a remedy to the complainant and cannot order the government department to do anything other than provide evidence and documents to assist with the investigation. So why bother complaining to the ombudsman in the first place? There are several reasons which belie the unfair characterization of ombudsmen as 'toothless tigers'. First, although an ombudsman report is not strictly binding on the government department subject to a complaint, the report will often make recommendations on what the department should do in a particular case or to avoid maladministration in the future. These recommendations are often implemented, not only because ombudsmen may have a good working relationship with government, but because government departments do not want the negative publicity that may be associated with detrimental findings in an ombudsman report. It would also be unfair to universally characterize public officials as careless in their approach to public service—the business of administering state services is complex and often made under significant resource pressures, so departments may welcome recommendations on how they can better deliver public services. Even in relation to a specific complaint received, an ombudsman may recommend the issuance of an apology, reconsideration of a decision, or payment of compensation, and the department may agree to do so. Second, an ombudsman can sometimes serve as a mediator, going back and forth between the complainant and the government department to try to find a solution. Sometimes a solution will indeed be found. More broadly, the ombudsman may be able to identify failings and recommend improvements in response to a public scandal.

The main ombudsman in the UK, known as the Parliamentary and Health Service Ombudsman (PHSO), was set up following the famous Crichel Down Affair. Land known as Crichel Down had been subject in 1938 to government compulsory purchase for war purposes. After the Second World War, Crichel Down was transferred to the Ministry of Agriculture, which revalued the land at an inflated price which was unaffordable to the original owners. The case was regarded as a major political scandal which resulted in a public inquiry and the creation of the ombudsman (or the 'Parliamentary Commissioner for Administration', as the office was technically known) in the UK in 1967, so that the ombudsman's very existence was in large measure the result of a public scandal.

Despite the general similarities among ombudsmen internationally, there are of course differences between them. Some legal systems, like Hong Kong, have a single, general ombudsman which handles a wide variety of complaints. Others, like the UK, have several, specialized ombudsmen in areas like health, prisons, and financial services. Federal systems tend either to have ombudsmen at both the federal and state level (as in Australia) or at the state level but not the federal level (as in Canada). The US is, as in many aspects of public law, something of an outlier in the common law world. It does not have a traditional ombudsman model: a number of states either have ombudsmen in their own right or more commonly as part of the governor's office, while there is no unified federal ombudsman other than the internal ombudsman functions of individual government agencies.

In many legal systems, ombudsmen are created by parliament. The fact that the ombudsman owes its existence to legislation in these systems means that it can be abolished by simple repeal of the legislation itself. This is true of the UK and Australia, for example, but is not true everywhere. An unusual case is Taiwan where the Control Yuan, a supervisory body that performs the ombudsman function in Taiwan, is enshrined in the Constitution. It is much more difficult to amend a constitution than legislation, so the Control Yuan has a significantly more entrenched legal footing in Taiwan than many ombudsmen found elsewhere. Some other countries also provide for ombudsmen in their constitutions, such as Finland, the Netherlands, and Thailand. Yet even when ombudsmen have a quite solid legal footing, they can suffer from a lack of proper resourcing such that they must turn away many complaints. If government wants to make an institution less effective without abolishing it, all it needs to do is turn off the money taps.

It is clear, however, that ombudsmen play an important role in securing government accountability in many systems which goes beyond matters of illegality which, apart from anything else, require someone with the willingness and resources to launch a legal action in court. In many cases litigation would also be out of all proportion to the nature of the complaint in question, and in that regard there is an increasing emphasis on the concept of 'proportionate dispute resolution' where the ombudsman has distinct advantages. It can therefore be seen that, even though ombudsmen cannot award directly enforceable remedies, they still have an important role to play in holding government to account. International cooperation among ombudsmen is facilitated by the International Ombudsman Institute headquartered in Vienna, Austria, representing over 200 ombudsman institutions from around the world.

Parliamentary complaints procedures

Parliaments often have systems in place whereby individuals can submit complaints to their parliamentary representatives about public administration. There is some degree of overlap between these complaints procedures and ombudsmen, and in fact ombudsmen have sometimes grown out of these procedures.

The classic example here is the UK's PHSO which still, after years of criticism, calls for change, and even a draft bill, uses an 'MP [Member of Parliament] filter'. This means that complaints to the PHSO (apart from health-related complaints) must come from an MP, so an individual must first complain to their MP before the complaint can reach the PHSO. The MP filter is seen as adding a barrier to the accessibility of the ombudsman and there is little to commend it, but it still shows the overlap between these two accountability channels. Nevertheless, constituents can complain to their MP directly about such diverse matters as education, health, or pensions provision, and MPs often have staff that include caseworkers who can take on individual complaints and attempt to resolve them. This could involve contacting a higher level official in a government department to bring an exceptional case to their attention, or directing the constituent to an organization which can take up their complaint.

Similar channels for making administrative complaints are found in other jurisdictions. In the US, complaints that have not been satisfactorily resolved by individual agencies can be referred to elected officials at the local (city or county), state, or federal

(House of Representatives or Senate) level. These officials have staff who can take up individual cases and liaise with government agencies on an individual's behalf. If, for example, an individual has an urgent problem which requires intervention by US Citizenship and Immigration Services (an agency of the US Department of Homeland Security), given that it is so difficult to speak to a human operator via their telephone line, an elected official's staff may be able to prompt an urgent response from an official working in that agency. Similarly, in Canada, an MP's staff can offer or facilitate more immediate support from a government department than may be possible by contacting the department directly. Contact with MPs is usually established remotely with their staff by mail, email, or telephone, but it can also be possible to meet the MP at their constituency office or when in the parliamentary capital.

Sometimes ombudsman and parliamentary complaints systems operate in parallel. An example is in Hong Kong where, alongside the Ombudsman, there is the Legislative Council Redress System which allows individuals to complain to their parliamentary representatives about government action. This is a more formalized parliamentary complaints procedure than simply directly contacting an elected representative. The Redress System in fact existed before the Ombudsman in Hong Kong, and part of its jurisdiction was transferred to the Ombudsman when the latter was established in 1989. What is interesting is that the Redress System was not abolished when the Ombudsman was created so that there are now two parallel channels for complaining about government action, though the Ombudsman is now the primary channel for making administrative complaints.

Parliamentary and congressional committees

Legislatures have another important role to play in administrative accountability. They often have committees, whose members are elected politicians, which scrutinize government action either generally or in relation to particular events. They have the power to call witnesses and take evidence on matters of importance affecting government action, and their proceedings can sometimes generate widespread media coverage and therefore accountability. Some committees, like the UK House of Commons Home Affairs Committee and the Canadian House of Commons Standing Committee on Health, are established committees with a permanent mandate (at least until they are changed or abolished), often attached to the work of a particular government department. Others, like the Australian Senate Select Committee on the Cost of Living and the Irish Joint Committee on Assisted Dying, are committees with a temporary mandate to investigate and report on a particular issue. In countries with bicameral parliaments, i.e. parliaments with two chambers or houses (including the UK, Canada, and Australia), committees can consist of members from both chambers—these are usually called joint committees.

The US Congress (consisting of the lower chamber, the House of Representatives; and the upper chamber, the Senate) uses a system of hearings in the process of policymaking and investigating matters of public concern. One of the most famous examples of such hearings was the Army–McCarthy hearings held in 1954 by the US Senate Permanent Subcommittee on Investigations. Wisconsin Senator Joseph McCarthy, who usually chaired the subcommittee but was on this occasion replaced by another senator, made legendary accusations about communist sympathizers in the US Army and government. The US Army, meanwhile, accused McCarthy of trying to blackmail it into a direct commission for a former aide. The hearings, which involved several dramatic exchanges, received widespread television coverage. They concluded that McCarthy had not tried improperly to influence the Army, but the hearings took a heavy toll on McCarthy's credibility and he was later censured by the Senate.

Another of the most famous hearings was the Watergate hearings. President Richard Nixon's administration had been involved in the burgling of the Democratic National Committee (DNC; the lead committee of the Democratic Party) headquarters in Washington, DC. The administration then tried to cover up its involvement. The US Senate Select Committee on Presidential Campaign Activities, also known as the Watergate Committee, sat from 1973 to 1974 to investigate the scandal. The hearings included a number of dramatic moments including testimony by former White House counsel, John Dean, that President Nixon personally knew about the cover-up of the burglary of the DNC headquarters, and testimony by former White House deputy assistant, Alexander Butterfield, that there was a secret White House taping system ordered by Nixon. The Watergate scandal, in which the Senate hearings played a major part, resulted in the resignation of Nixon from the US presidency.

A further and more recent high-profile hearing was the US House Select Committee on Events Surrounding the 2012 Terrorist Attack in Benghazi. The work of the committee ran from 2014 to 2016 and concluded among other things that the US State Department had failed to protect US diplomats in Libya, that Hillary Clinton (who was the US Secretary of State at the time of the Benghazi attacks) failed to realize and address the risks posed to those diplomats, and that Clinton had deleted emails from a private server that she was using for official business which subverted the work of the committee. Clinton's behaviour with regard to her emails and the private server were seized upon, and arguably successfully exploited, by Donald Trump in their electoral contest for the US presidency in 2016. Each of these three, high-profile examples shows the kind of political consequences that can be generated by such congressional hearings.

Another example which UK readers might remember was the appearance of politician George Galloway MP before the Senate Permanent Subcommittee on Investigations to investigate alleged

6. Hillary Clinton appears before the US House Select Committee on Events Surrounding the 2012 Terrorist Attack in Benghazi, Washington, DC, USA.

abuses of the UN's Oil-for-Food Program. Galloway made headlines in 2005 for his barnstorming appearance before the hearings to which he was summoned on the allegation that he had participated in Program abuses, and was also notable because he was at the time a sitting MP in a foreign parliament.

Of course, the work of parliamentary committees is not always so notorious. But they play an important role in scrutinizing the work of government ministers and departments, shining a light on issues and putting questions to officials, and being able to report and make recommendations on appropriate solutions to particular problems. They also, depending on the remit of the committee, play a role in policy formulation because they can often scrutinize bills as part of the broader lawmaking process. Additionally, as these committees are made up of elected politicians but operate in a less adversarial format than the main parliamentary chamber, their work is often (but not always) less politically charged and more deliberative. The nuances of technical discussions are also more likely to be appropriately ventilated in parliamentary committees than in the main parliamentary chamber.

Public inquiries

Public inquiries are often set up following public scandals or negative events of major public interest. They can be set up under legislation or by executive order and have varying powers—for example, some have powers to take evidence under oath, while others do not. Their purpose is usually a fact-finding exercise in response to something that has gone seriously wrong in public administration, either because of the nature of what has happened or the number of people affected, and to make recommendations on how a repeat can be avoided. They sometimes apportion blame to particular government departments or officials but many refer instead to broader systemic failings.

The work of inquiries can span a number of years depending on the scale and complexity of their work. Some notable examples of inquiries set up in the UK in recent years include:

Iraq Inquiry ('Chilcot Inquiry')	2009–16
Historical Institutional Abuse Inquiry	2012–17
Grenfell Tower Inquiry	2017–24
Infected Blood Inquiry	2017–24
Manchester Arena Inquiry	2019–23
Post Office Horizon IT Inquiry	2020–present
UK COVID-19 Inquiry	2022–present

Similarly, recent notable examples of Royal Commissions in Australia—the highest form of public inquiry in that country—include:

7. Paula Vennells, former chief executive officer of Post Office Ltd, appears before the Post Office Horizon IT Inquiry in London, UK.

Royal Commission into Institutional Responses to Child Sexual Abuse	2013–17
Royal Commission into Misconduct in the Banking, Superannuation and Financial Services Industry ('Hayne Royal Commission')	2017–19
Royal Commission into Violence, Abuse, Neglect and Exploitation of People with Disability	2019–present
Royal Commission into National Natural Disaster Arrangements	2020–20
Royal Commission into the Robodebt Scheme	2022–3

The UK's Infected Blood Inquiry is a good example of how a public inquiry can be set up to investigate and respond to a widespread or serious failure in public administration. From around 1970 onwards, tens of thousands of National Health Service (NHS) patients had been given blood, blood products, or tissue that was infected with human immunodeficiency virus

(HIV) or one or more hepatitis viruses. Around 26,800 people alone were infected with Hepatitis C after a blood transfusion related to childbirth, surgery, or treatment of sickle cell disease or other conditions More than 3,000 people died as a result of receiving infected blood, blood products, or tissue; thousands more suffered serious physical and psychological injuries. To investigate how this happened, its impact, and whether there had been a cover-up, the Infected Blood Inquiry was set up in 2017 and issued its 2,527-page report in 2024.

The inquiry found that a large number of failures had led to the mass infection of NHS patients and inappropriate responses to that. Factors leading to the infection of people with blood disorders included failures in the licensing regime on blood products, failures to make adjustments to treatment regimes to make them safer, and conducting research on people without informing them beforehand. Factors leading to the infections of people who received blood transfusions included failures to ensure sufficiently careful and rigorous donor selection and screening, delaying screening of blood donations, and giving more transfusions than was clinically required. In relation to both groups of people, the inquiry found that the NHS and clinicians were, among other things, complacent about the risks of Hepatitis C and slow to respond to the risks of AIDS, failed to tell people of the risks of treatment or transfusions, failed to seek consent on a properly informed basis, delayed informing people that they were infected by weeks, months, or even years, and failed to properly keep medical records.

More broadly, the inquiry found, among other things, repeated and ongoing failures to acknowledge that people should not have been infected, an absence of any meaningful apology or redress, 'a lack of openness, transparency and candour, shown by the NHS and government, such that the truth has been hidden for decades', deliberate destruction of documents, failures to appropriately support infected persons, and refusals to provide compensation.

The inquiry made a number of recommendations in its report, from specific clinical care recommendations to increased accountability of persons in leadership positions within the NHS. But the principal recommendation was that a compensation scheme be established immediately. Within months, compensation regulations had been approved by Parliament.

The work of a public inquiry can, within obvious limits, lead to improved outcomes for people affected by scandals or widespread failures of public administration, address broader systemic, resource, or cultural problems, and reduce the probability that similar failures occur again in the future. It can also increase transparency and accountability in government and public administration.

However, there are limitations to the potential of public inquiries and risks in how they are set up and run. The Iraq Inquiry was criticized in terms of who had been (and had not been) appointed by the government to the Inquiry Committee, that there were political dimensions to the timing of the inquiry's operations, that key evidence was blocked or suppressed including material that might prove damaging to UK–US relations, and that the inquiry took an excessive length of time to publish its report. All of this can be compared with a court of law which is better insulated against this kind of (alleged) external control and interference. But it must be remembered that courts only exist to determine questions of legality and public inquiries can look not only at issues of legality but also broader questions of good public administration and government. Public inquiries are therefore a broader piece of the accountability jigsaw, but it is also worth pointing out that the setting up of a public inquiry can be a way of politicians kicking the can down the road—these inquiries often take years to set up, operate, and issue a report, by which time the relevant holders of political office may well have departed and the issues of the day may have moved on. They can also be expensive to run: the Infected Blood Inquiry cost over £140 million, while the UK's Saville Inquiry (the 'Bloody Sunday Inquiry') cost over £210 million.

Human rights monitors

Some countries have a dedicated human rights agency. The standard model is for there to be a commission comprising a number of commissioners. For example, the Australian Human Rights Commission is a national human rights oversight body with a number of commissioners with individual responsibilities, spanning human rights in general, children's welfare, privacy, discrimination on the basis of age, disability, race, and sex, and Aboriginal and Torres Strait Islander social justice. The commission investigates violations of rules in these areas by federal government agencies. Some states like Victoria have their own human rights agency, while others like New South Wales do not. The UK has an Equality and Human Rights Commission which (though established by the Equality Act 2006) enforces the Equality Act 2010 across nine 'protected characteristics'—age, disability, gender reassignment, marriage and civil partnership, pregnancy and maternity, race, religion or belief, sex, and sexual orientation. Like its Australian counterpart, the UK's commission has a number of commissioners but they do not have individual portfolios. Canada, too, has its own Canadian Human Rights Commission. The work of these bodies often finds traction in the employment field but not exclusively so; for example, discrimination in the provision of public services can also be targeted.

These bodies are part of the administrative law apparatus because they are the monitoring and/or enforcement arm of these regulatory frameworks. The UK's Equality and Human Rights Commission, for example, has the power to investigate bodies that may be in non-compliance with their legal obligations in this field and to issue compliance notices against public bodies that are failing to uphold their legal duties. Similarly, the commission can launch or intervene in judicial review proceedings. The Australian and Canadian equivalents also have enforcement powers.

However, not all human rights monitors have enforcement powers. The remit of the US Commission on Civil Rights covers similar areas—deprivation of voting rights and alleged discrimination on the basis of race, colour, religion, sex, age, disability, and national origin, or in the administration of justice—but it does not have direct enforcement powers. Instead, it operates like an ombudsman in these areas by investigating and reporting on alleged violations. The National Human Rights Commission of India also does not have enforcement powers, but is chaired by a person who has been a Chief Justice of India or a judge of the Supreme Court, and has other members including the chairpersons of various national commissions, such as the National Commission for Protection of Child Rights, the National Commission for Scheduled Castes, and the National Commission for Backward Classes.

While equality of opportunity and absence of discrimination are laudable objectives, there are risks to enshrining these in the form of 'protected characteristics'. One is the politicized nature of deciding which characteristics are protected. Absent from the UK's nine characteristics, for example, are a number of characteristics that some have argued should be included: socio-economic class, education, general health, menopause, and political opinion to name just a few. It can indeed be difficult to justify the inclusion of some of these characteristics and the omission of others. However, the more characteristics that are protected, the broader and more general the prohibitions on discrimination become, in which case should human rights instead be enforced on broader bases such as human dignity and freedom of choice, or would these be too broad and vague to enforce? Another challenge is that protected characteristics can clash, such as when a workplace adopts a particular stance on sexuality which conflicts with the religious beliefs of some employees.

Around 120 national human rights institutions are members of the Global Alliance of National Human Rights Institutions (GANHRI) which promotes human rights principles and compliance with the UN's Paris Principles on human rights. This also serves an accreditation function which allows individual human rights institutions to be granted access to the UN Human Rights Council.

Anti-corruption bodies

Corruption can take many different forms. Bribery, fraud, money laundering, smuggling, trafficking, embezzlement, kickbacks, influence peddling, and rigging are among its many guises. Corruption can exist in all branches of the state. A government official might grant permits or award lucrative procurement contracts based on personal connections or financial interests. A legislator might vote for a bill due to a payment received from a lobbyist. A judge might decide a case in favour of a party who has promised to make a payment to them or issued a threat against the judge or their family members.

A high-profile example of corruption was the UK parliamentary expenses scandal that emerged in 2009. MPs are permitted to claim expenses in connection with costs incurred 'wholly, exclusively, and necessarily' in the performance of their parliamentary duties. Journalists made FOI requests to investigate actual MP expenses, but this was resisted by the House of Commons, and the (Labour) leader of the House of Commons tabled a motion to exempt MP expenses from FOI disclosure. This was dropped in the face of significant opposition, and a number of scandals were revealed both before and after the proposal was axed. These included widespread practices such as 'flipping' second homes so that MPs could claim purchase and renovation costs for more than one property, overclaiming council tax, and exploitation of a rule that claims below £250 did not require receipts to be submitted. Individual examples of egregious expenditure included a Conservative MP who claimed £30,000 of gardening expenses including £1,645 for a 'duck island', and a Labour MP and government minister who claimed expenses for a second home, occupied by his parents, which was only eight miles from his main residence. Some of this activity was unlawful, with seven MPs imprisoned for false accounting and/or mortgage fraud, but other practices were technically permitted by parliamentary rules and simply exploited. As a result of the scandal, the Independent Parliamentary Standards Authority (IPSA) was created by the UK Parliament to regulate MPs' pay and expenses in a more independent and impartial manner.

Corruption can be a costly diversion of public funds and resources. In the UK, an enormous £21 billion is estimated by the UK Parliament's Public Accounts Committee to have been lost in pandemic fraud, roughly equivalent to the cost of building 42 new hospitals. It should need little explanation why corruption is a bad thing, with damaging effects on the rule of law, democracy, fairness, equality, accountability, and efficiency in public spending. As part of an international attempt to stamp out corruption, the Organisation for Economic Co-operation and Development (OECD) Anti-Bribery Convention was signed in 1997 and currently has 46 parties. Though some of its signatories are recognized as international leaders in the anti-corruption field, such as Denmark, Finland, and New Zealand (which led the most recent Corruption Perceptions Index published by Transparency International), it also includes countries that are very poorly regarded in terms of corruption, such as Brazil, Mexico, and Russia (which are poorly scored in the Corruption Perceptions Index).

Many anti-corruption efforts took their inspiration from the US Foreign Corrupt Practices Act of 1977, which illegalized payments by US citizens and entities to foreign officials to benefit their own business interests. One of the most brazen examples of corruption in the US in the 20th century was under the administration of President Warren G. Harding, whose Secretary of the Interior leased petroleum reserves in Wyoming to oil companies at below-market prices without a competitive bidding process. The Secretary was convicted of accepting bribes from those oil companies and was imprisoned. Later, President Richard Nixon was implicated in various corruption allegations, the most famous of which was the Watergate scandal. Often, regulatory progress is made in response to scandals, and the enactment of the Foreign Corrupt Practices Act followed a number of scandals involving bribery of foreign officials. Nowadays, the US does not have a dedicated anti-corruption agency, but the function is shared among several agencies including the Federal Bureau of Investigation (FBI), the Internal Revenue Service—Criminal Investigation, and an agency's Office of the Inspector General.

Canada also does not have a dedicated anti-corruption agency—the anti-corruption function is instead fulfilled by the police. However, many countries have a dedicated agency tasked with fighting corruption. In the UK, the anti-corruption function is mainly vested in the Serious Fraud Office, which has the power to both investigate and prosecute offences. It is operationally supported by the police and the National Crime Agency, such as where search and arrest powers are needed. In Australia, the function is fulfilled by the National Anti-Corruption Commission, though the commission does not have the power to make findings of criminality; instead, it makes referrals to the Commonwealth Director of Public Prosecutions who will decide whether the case merits prosecution. As Australia is a federal country, there are also anti-corruption agencies at the state and territory level—the first of these was established in 1989 in New South Wales and the most recent was established in 2018 in the Northern Territory. In India, the main anti-corruption agency is the Central Vigilance Commission, with a role also played by the Central Bureau of

Investigation. India is also a federal country and some of its states have their own anti-corruption agencies, in addition to the Lokayukta for each state which shares ombudsman and anti-corruption functions.

The overlap between ombudsman and anti-corruption functions is also found elsewhere. For example, in Macau—a former Portuguese colony and now one of the People's Republic of China's two Special Administrative Regions—the two functions are combined in the Commission Against Corruption (CCAC) which is embedded in Macau's Basic Law (its 'mini-constitution'). Yet in China's other Special Administrative Region, Hong Kong—a former British colony—the two functions are kept separate. The ombudsman function is performed by the Ombudsman and the anti-corruption function is performed by the Independent Commission Against Corruption (ICAC). The ICAC is embedded in Hong Kong's Basic Law, but the Ombudsman is not.

8. Praveen Kumar Srivastava (far left) is sworn in as the Central Vigilance Commissioner, New Delhi, India.

This means that in Hong Kong the Ombudsman could be abolished by ordinary legislation, but the ICAC could not. In Macau, the CCAC could not be abolished by ordinary legislation, and as the CCAC also performs an ombudsman function, we can see that the ombudsman function is constitutionally protected in one of China's Special Administrative Regions but not in the other. And interestingly, the two functions can come into conflict: in 2024, Chris Field resigned as the Western Australian Ombudsman following a finding of serious misconduct against him by the state's Corruption and Crime Commission for alleged excessive overseas travel spending and misallocation of resources in connection with his tenure as President of the International Ombudsman Institute.

Public service integrity bodies

There are miscellaneous other bodies that seek to uphold integrity in public service. These overlap with anti-corruption and financial integrity functions depending on the country involved, but they also include whistleblower protection agencies, election commissions, civil service discipline commissions, and other bodies that help to maintain public confidence in government.

The US has a long tradition of whistleblowing, with famous whistleblowers including W. Mark Felt, Chelsea Manning, and Edward Snowden. Felt, better known as 'Deep Throat', was an associate director of the FBI who leaked information during the Watergate scandal which ultimately resulted in the resignation of President Richard Nixon. Manning, a US Army intelligence specialist, who released the largest set of classified documents on record primarily to WikiLeaks, was imprisoned for violating the Espionage Act of 1917. Snowden, a Booz Allen Hamilton contractor to the National Security Agency, leaked highly classified information having fled to Hong Kong and then Russia. Whistleblowers play an important part in securing accountability in the public sector, exposing malpractice, illegality, scandals, or extreme waste within government. There is often a public interest in their speaking out and revealing things which might otherwise never be known to the public. But there is also a public interest in ensuring that government insiders do not freely leak information to all and sundry, which could ultimately be damaging to national security or stability. So again there is a difficult balance to be struck.

Whistleblower protection legislation grants certain protections to those who choose to speak out. The US enacted the Whistleblower Protection Act of 1989 which aims to protect whistleblowers from retaliatory measures taken against them by public agencies. The Office of Special Counsel and the Merit Systems Protection Board have the power to investigate and adjudicate whistleblower complaints, while the Court of Appeals for the Federal Circuit hears appeals from the Merit Systems Protection Board.

Whistleblower protections are also found elsewhere. The Office of the Public Sector Integrity Commissioner of Canada was established in 2007 to investigate wrongdoing in the federal public sector and protect whistleblowers from reprisals. The commissioner's task is to investigate complaints of reprisals against public servants who have chosen to speak out, with cases where reprisal is deemed to have been established referred to a tribunal. The commissioner does, however, have broader jurisdiction that does not only apply in whistleblower cases. Meanwhile, the Public Service Commission of Canada oversees standards in the appointment of civil servants and maintenance of their integrity.

A recent notable case in Australia demonstrates the difficult issues which are at play with regard to whistleblowers. David McBride, who was a lawyer for the Australian Army, leaked classified military documents to the media which indicated that war crimes may have taken place in Afghanistan at the hands of Australian elite special forces. McBride pleaded guilty to state secrets offences after his claims to protection under whistleblower legislation were ruled to be ineffective due to national security risks. McBride had argued that he leaked the documents in the public interest and to secure accountability within the Australian military, but his criminal conviction has led some to argue that Australian whistleblower protections are not sufficiently strong.

Public service integrity is not just about protecting whistleblowers. There are often bodies which enforce codes of conduct against public servants to ensure that public trust is upheld in the work of government. In the UK, the Civil Service Commission hears complaints from civil servants under the Civil Service Code, which forms part of the engagement conditions of every civil servant, and promotes the Code in conjunction with government departments. The Code includes provisions about civil servant impartiality, honesty, and objectivity, among others. Ultimately, a civil servant can be dismissed for acting in violation of the Code. Many countries also have bodies which investigate complaints about the police, allegations of police misconduct, or circumstances where a person dies or is seriously injured following contact with the police. These include England and Wales's Independent Office for Police Conduct, Canada's Civilian Review and Complaints Commission for the Royal Canadian Mounted Police, Hong Kong's Independent Police Complaints Council, and police complaints authorities in several Indian states. These bodies are often independent of police forces and may only become involved if internal police complaints procedures are exhausted or found to be deficient. They sometimes also perform an auditing function of the fairness, propriety, and effectiveness of internal police complaints procedures.

There is also an anti-corruption function at play in the work of some public integrity institutions, whether within the work of government or to ensure the democratic integrity of elections. There are clearly risks for the democratic credentials of elections if they are run or supervised directly by the government, so to ensure fair play, including in how election campaigns are financed, it is often a good idea to have an independent election commission which enforces rules and standards in this area. The Public Integrity Section of the US Department of Justice plays an anti-corruption function but also prosecutes election crimes and alleged criminal conduct by federal judges. The Federal Election Commission (which is an independent agency of the US government) plays its own role in election integrity by enforcing campaign finance rules. For example, it acted on a complaint received about Sam Bankman-Fried, founder of cryptocurrency exchange FTX, for alleged campaign finance violations relating to the donation of tens of millions of dollars to political campaigns. Meanwhile, the UK's Electoral Commission is its independent agency for enforcing election campaign rules and regulating standards in the running of elections. In Ireland, an Electoral Commission was not established until 2023, despite being in the offing for many years before. The Election Commission of India is protected by the Indian Constitution.

Financial integrity and public audit bodies

The idea of a public official responsible for auditing government spending has a long history. In England, there was an Auditor of the Exchequer as long ago as 1314. But things have come a long way and financial integrity and public audit bodies can now be put into two categories: independent audit bodies and parliamentary accounts committees.

The first type comprises independent audit bodies such as the UK National Audit Office, the US Government Accountability Office, and the Australian National Audit Office. In federal countries like Australia and Canada, there are similar bodies at the state level, and in the UK there are similar bodies at the devolved level in Scotland, Wales, and Northern Ireland. These bodies tend to be independent of government and funded by and/or accountable to parliaments. Their functions often include auditing public accounts for accuracy, fairness, and legality, and making assessments about whether public funding meets 'value for money' benchmarks. These bodies are often headed by a public official called 'auditor-general' (as in Australia, Canada, and Ghana), 'comptroller-general' (as in the US), or a combination of the two (as in the UK, Ireland, and India). The independent bodies and/or the leading officials of such bodies tend to have their legal foundation in legislation in common law countries, though sometimes they are mentioned in the national constitution—for example, the Office of Auditor-General in Ghana is enshrined in its Constitution.

National audit institutions are known as 'supreme audit institutions' and they are members of the International Organization of Supreme Audit Institutions (INTOSAI), founded in Cuba in 1953 and now headquartered in Austria. INTOSAI serves three main functions: facilitating international standardization of supreme audit functions as through the publication of the INTOSAI Auditing Standards; facilitating cooperation among and capacity building in supreme audit institutions; and serving as the main external auditor of the UN.

Independent audit bodies are sometimes complemented by fiscal councils, which are defined by the International Monetary Fund as 'permanent agenc[ies] with a statutory or executive mandate to assess publicly and independently from partisan influence government's fiscal policies, plans and performance against macroeconomic objectives related to the long-term sustainability of public finances, short-medium-term macroeconomic stability, and other official objectives'. There are currently 49 countries with fiscal councils, most of them created in the 21st century. These include Canada's Parliamentary Budget Office (2008), the UK's Office for Budget Responsibility (2010), and Australia's Parliamentary Budget Office (2012). However, some fiscal councils have a longer history, including the US's Congressional Budget Office (1974), and the world's oldest extant fiscal council is the Netherlands Bureau for Economic Policy Analysis (1945).

The second type of body comprises parliamentary accounts committees. Although we have already discussed parliamentary committees earlier in this chapter, it is important to point out that parliaments often have committees specifically designed to ensure accountability in public spending. The task of the UK House of Commons Public Accounts Committee, for example, is to 'examine the value for money of Government projects, programmes and service delivery' and '[d]rawing on the work of the National Audit Office the Committee holds government officials to account for the economy, efficiency and effectiveness of public spending'. Similarly, the work of the Canadian House of Commons Standing Committee on Public Accounts is framed in the following terms:

> Under the Westminster-style legislative tradition that Canada inherited from the United Kingdom, a government cannot spend public monies or raise taxes without first seeking and securing the explicit consent of Parliament. It is also necessary to ensure that these funds have been spent in the amounts and for the purpose specified by the authorization. Thus, some form of public accounting and auditing must be undertaken to ensure that Parliament's intentions have been respected. That accounting and auditing role has traditionally been carried out by a public accounts committee.

Like committees in other countries include the Australian Joint Committee of Public Accounts and Audit, the Irish Committee of Public Accounts, and the New Zealand Finance and Expenditure Committee.

But why have both types of institution: independent audit bodies and parliamentary accounts committees? Independent audit bodies, which typically comply with recognized accounting and auditing standards such as the INTOSAI Auditing Standards, conduct a more technical auditing of public spending. That information is then available to parliamentary accounts committees which can then hold government to account by inviting government ministers and officials to appear before them to explain anomalies or problems with the audited accounts or instances of public spending. So independent audit bodies really perform a supporting function in the political process by giving parliamentary committees the information they need to act as a check on government power in the field of public spending.

Regulators

Where administrative law ends and other areas of law begin is a difficult question. There are myriad bodies regulating such diverse areas as broadcasting, medicines, pensions, social housing, education, energy, and gambling. Many of these entities are the enforcement arm of complex bodies of law regulating these specialist areas. Examples include NHS England, the Australian Energy Regulator, the New Zealand Financial Markets Authority, and the Irish Environmental Protection Agency. Some of these sit within government departments but with significant independence and autonomy, while others sit outside of government, such as UK 'non-departmental public bodies' (like NHS England).

Often regulators will have powers to issue binding rules or standards (of major significance in the US), operate licensing systems, hear complaints against regulated bodies, and impose fines or sanctions on regulated bodies. In this way they occupy a grey area in the public law field. They can make rules, but are not legislators in the sense of parliaments (and, for that matter, are usually set up by parliaments as statutory authorities). They can adjudicate complaints and/or disputes and impose sanctions, but are not courts. They might in some situations operate like tribunals, attracting rules of procedural fairness that apply to those bodies. They are, if given a straight choice between legislature, executive, and judiciary, part of the executive, but often operate quite independently of government. Indeed, part of the reason for keeping regulatory bodies at arm's length from the government is that government ministers can avoid some of the accountability for activities that, but for the establishment of the independent regulator, would have been performed by the government itself. While this tends to be justified on the basis that the regulator will be protected from 'political interference' when things do go wrong, it is easier to blame the regulator which was at arm's length from the government and left to get on with the task itself.

There is a paradox at play here. The general trajectory over the decades is one of an increase in the size of government and the reach of its regulatory tentacles. At the same time, there are more arm's length regulatory bodies than ever carrying out much of the work of government. This can generate a real accountability gap, not only between members of the public and regulators, but between elected officials and regulators, because many of these regulators are not subject to direct government departmental control. When government ministers want to re-exert control, they may bring the regulatory powers back into a government department, perhaps abolishing the arm's length regulator altogether. This happened with the UK Border Agency, which was abolished as an arm's length body and its work returned to the Home Office, and the Australian National Preventive Health Agency, which was abolished and its work transferred to the Department of Health.

Freedom of information bodies

'Open government is part of effective democracy', once said a UK government policy paper. The idea is fairly simple: how can we secure accountability in government when so many decisions, processes, and policies are not in the public domain? How do we know what is happening behind those gated cloisters and hallowed walls? But it goes beyond democracy to the rule of law itself. How can we challenge decisions when information relevant to those decisions is withheld? What policies and procedures are used when making decisions which might affect us? Parliaments in various countries have enacted legislation to allow individuals to apply for information to be released by public bodies and thus improve transparency in government. These include the US's Freedom of Information Act of 1967 (FOIA), Australia's Freedom of Information Act 1982, New Zealand's Official Information Act 1982, Canada's Access to Information Act 1985, and the UK's Freedom of Information Act 2000. In federal countries like Australia, Canada, and the US, there is also equivalent FOI legislation at the state and territory level.

There is a difficult balancing act to pull off here. There can be legitimate public interest reasons why governments do not want information to be released. These include security reasons and information which could prejudice legal processes, public procurement decisions, commercial arrangements, and information which could complicate foreign affairs. But there is also information that governments might not want us to know and which it is in the public interest to disclose: skeletons in the closet, evidence of waste, inefficiency, incompetence, or scandal. Governments mainly raise money through taxation and that comes from members of the public. We are, in principle, entitled to know how our tax dollars are being wasted, squandered, or handled incompetently or scandalously. With this information we can demand accountability of government ministers, school authorities, or hospital managers. We can get issues into the media or into the local, regional, or national conversation. We can conclude that a particular political party is not fit for government and be better informed so as to cast our votes differently at the next election. If governments are there to serve us, the people, then we are entitled to know what governments are doing in our name and with our money. That is the fundamental justification for FOI laws.

In the US, over 1.1 million FOIA requests were made in fiscal year 2023, not even including requests at the state level. There were 34,797 FOI requests made in Australia in the most recent annualized figures, again only at the federal level. In the most recently available statistics, there were 52,740 FOI requests made annually in the UK, the largest number of requests on record in that country. When a government body receives an FOI request, it must commit resources to determining whether the request is valid and one that it is legally obliged to fulfil. If it is, it will have to commit more resources to finding and collating the information requested. The legislation can stipulate limits on the maximum that a public authority is obliged to spend before it can decline to fulfil some or all of the FOI request; in the UK that is £600 for a central government department and £450 for other public authorities. And the costs of this exercise add up. It is difficult to obtain figures for the overall cost to the public purse of FOI requests, but almost 20 years ago research showed that this cost UK taxpayers £35.5 million in a single year.

It might be argued that this is a price worth paying for more transparent government. Enhanced democracy and the rule of law comes at a cost. But Tony Blair, who was the Prime Minister who oversaw the introduction of FOI legislation in the UK, would later have this to say about it in his autobiography:

> Freedom of information. Three harmless words. I look at these words as I write them, and feel like shaking my head till it drops off my shoulders. You idiot. You naive, foolish, irresponsible nincompoop. There is really no description of stupidity, no matter how vivid, that is adequate. I quake at the imbecility of it.

Why the change of heart? Blair went on:

> The truth is that the FOI Act isn't used, for the most part, by 'the people'. It's used by journalists. For political leaders, it's like

saying to someone who is hitting you over the head with a stick, 'Hey, try this instead', and handing them a mallet. The information is neither sought because the journalist is curious to know, nor given to bestow knowledge on 'the people'. It's used as a weapon.

This perception may explain why some of the author's own FOI requests have initially been met with the imperative from the public authority: 'please confirm that you are not a journalist'. Though, under the legislation, journalists are as entitled as anyone else to submit FOI requests.

FOI legislation tends to have exceptions to some of the information already identified as more problematic for release—information concerning national security, foreign relations, commercial partnerships, advice to governments from their legal advisors, or information which might jeopardize investigations or law enforcement. While these and the various other exemptions that are available may sound reasonable and often will be reasonable, it will sometimes be the case that the public body, which ultimately must determine whether an exemption does or does not apply, is overzealous and categorizes information as exempt when it should not be so categorized.

In those types of situations, the legislation can be enforced by an oversight body like the UK's Information Commissioner's Office, which also has responsibility for data protection and privacy issues. There are similar bodies elsewhere, such as the Office of the Australian Information Commissioner, Canada's Office of the Information Commissioner, and Ireland's Information Commissioner. These bodies typically have rule-making and enforcement powers, and also issue codes of practice for public bodies to follow. A slightly different approach is adopted in New Zealand, where the Ombudsman is the enforcer of FOI obligations rather than a dedicated information commissioner.

Ultimately, statutory duties can of course be enforced in a court. This happened in the famous 'Black Spider Memos' case which began life with a journalist submitting an FOI request for various letters and memos sent by the then Prince Charles to UK government ministers. The public interest in seeing such letters was to assess whether and to what extent Prince Charles, who was heir apparent to the throne which constitutionally requires political neutrality, was influencing government decision making. The government refused to release the letters by invoking exemptions on constitutional grounds, but the dispute, which proceeded via the Information Commissioner and the Upper Tribunal, was resolved when the UK Supreme Court ruled in *R (on the application of Evans) v Attorney General* [2015] UKSC 21 that the letters must be disclosed under the Freedom of Information Act 2000.

Chapter 6
The future of administrative law

Administrative law does not operate in a vacuum. It is shaped by the world around it—politics, economics, science, technology, social factors. Law also has a tendency to be responsive to societal events. Anti-terrorism legislation is usually enacted in response to acts of terrorism. Policing legislation is usually enacted in response to some event or trend revealing inadequacies in police powers or resourcing. Cryptocurrency regulations are being enacted in response to the emergence and growth of cryptocurrencies. Artificial intelligence (AI) is comparatively barely regulated at all, and there are calls for regulation of this field before something happens that has far-reaching effects socially, economically, politically, or even existentially. Administrative law lags behind societal developments in the way that most areas of law do; that is historically how it has developed. The question is what the future of administrative law looks like in an age of multiple, serious challenges on all these fronts.

In Chapter 3, we discussed some of the problems associated with the muddying of the waters between the public sector and the private sector, such as with private companies running prisons, conducting welfare benefits assessments, and operating public hospitals. How does administrative law need to adapt to these changing realities of government? How can it ensure that accountability is not weakened or lost altogether when the private sector plays such a key role in public service delivery? How should it deal with situations where public bodies—which are under a duty to act in the public interest and must remain free to do so—bind themselves to commercial contracts that limit their freedom to do just that? For example, a public health authority might sign a contract with a private company to build and operate a public hospital for a period of 25 years. The contract might stipulate that the authority must pay substantial financial penalties if it reneges on its contractual obligations, or it might be prohibited from reneging on them altogether. It might no longer be in the public interest for the health authority to be locked into this contract (for example, the payment of an annual sum to the private company might now be unaffordable due to broader economic conditions), but is it in the public interest for the health authority to be required to pay out substantial financial penalties for reneging on its contractual obligations? What has, and what should, administrative law to say about that? None of this is hypothetical. Europe's largest local authority, Birmingham City Council, was embroiled in years of legal wrangling with Amey plc which was contracted to maintain the area's roads over a 25-year period.

There is a broader resource problem which has extensive implications for administrative law. Many public service providers are groaning under unsustainable resource pressures. Birmingham City Council, which delivers many local public services to over a million people, effectively went bankrupt in 2023. Other local authorities are also regarded as at high risk of running out of money. NHS waiting lists are at record levels and growing. Taxpayers enquiring about or challenging tax bills can sit in telephone waiting queues for hours or even be unable to speak with a human operator: almost one million telephone calls to HMRC went unanswered in January 2024 alone. The UK House of Commons Public Accounts Committee reported in early 2024 that 'HMRC's customer service levels are at an all-time low because of conscious choices made by HMRC and HM Treasury'. HMRC announced shortly afterwards that its self-assessment telephone helpline—which received three million calls in 2023—would be closed for three months every summer to allow 'helpline advisors to focus support where it is most needed' and to push enquiries online. That of course assumes that online enquiry processes are adequate and that telephone support is not where support is most needed—highly contestable claims. Tellingly, the Chancellor of the Exchequer then ordered this change to be 'halted', with the HMRC Chief Executive subsequently stating that their 'helpline and webchat advisers will always be there for those taxpayers who need support because they are vulnerable, digitally excluded or have complex affairs'.

Not only do exacerbated resource constraints result in poorer public service delivery and a decrease in accountability, some public bodies are increasingly unable to meet their statutory obligations. There is thus a growing divide not only between what public authorities are able to provide in terms of services and what the public demands of them, but between what they are able to provide and what the *law* requires of them. It perhaps does not help matters that the law requires ever more of them. Throwing additional money at the problem does not seem to be an effective or a sustainable answer; that has been tried, and the problem is, if anything, worse.

In addition, we looked in Chapter 5 at independent regulators: is this burgeoning sector the right model for regulation of many areas of public and private life, or is it introducing too much bureaucracy, inefficiency, unaccountability, and cost into our societies? And then we have the access to justice problem: what good is judicial review—vital as it is—if few people can afford to take a public body to court? Legal aid systems are notoriously underfunded and, frankly, unaffordable if they were to be expanded to their necessary extent. It is all very well to be sure that a public body has acted unlawfully by violating its statutory or common law duties, quite another to go to court to enforce that. And if an aggrieved person cannot afford to go to court, the public body may well continue as before with the same unfairness or illegality carrying on.

The question then becomes how administrative law remains relevant in societies hamstrung by high inflation, cost-of-living crises, and increasingly scarce resources. It is tempting to think that administrative law on the books and administrative law in practice experience a growing divide. We have explored in this book how administrative tribunals, ombudsmen, human rights monitors, and public inquiries all have an important role to play in delivering administrative law accountability, but all of this has to be paid for. Can countries with increasingly unsustainable public finances afford to do so? The UK's Saville Inquiry (the 'Bloody Sunday Inquiry') cost over £210 million alone. Do these inquiries represent value for money? Is their cost proportionate to the benefits they bestow? Are they a luxury we can decreasingly afford? Or are they so crucial to the rule of law and political accountability that we must retain them at all costs? Are individuals, for whom the cost of access to justice is problematic, increasingly turning to crowdfunding or AI tools for 'legal advice', and what implications might that have for accountability?

This feeds into a broader issue which is a lack of public trust in public institutions. Public trust in elected politicians seems to ever recede and a polarization in public opinion is readily apparent. It is not that people were not polarized before, but that social media and the rise of non-traditional media amplify not only the polarized viewpoints but their political and social effects. As the public seem ever more disdainful and dismissive of elected politicians, will they also turn on courts, tribunals, regulators, and other institutions of administrative law? In some ways they already are. When the outcomes of Supreme Court cases (as in relation to Brexit) or the setting up or conclusions of public inquiries are regarded as an establishment stitch-up, trust in the rule of law and democracy itself can start to come loose. Growing disenfranchisement and disgruntlement can lead to public disorder and a desire for radical solutions. As is often the case, it is typically the middle ground that represents the more likely scenario: these outcomes are probably not an establishment conspiracy, but nor are concerns about accountability and representation baseless. The more likely explanation is incompetence, bad management, overcomplexity, unaffordability, and poor regulatory and policy choices which lead to systems not working in the way that they should. Much of government is about firefighting rather than unassailably improving living standards. Administrative law is often a firefighting exercise. The question is whether administrative law in its current form can cope with the intensifying scale and nature of the blaze.

Administrative law, whether at a national or local level, is not insulated from wider global events. The greatest global disruption in the early 21st century has been the COVID-19 pandemic, which brought a global shutdown of travel, infrastructure, and social interaction unparalleled in the modern era. The law seemed largely to be overtaken by events, with ordinary law and law-making processes to a greater or lesser extent overridden by 'states of emergency' and a massive increase in centralized executive control. Administrative (and other areas of) law must be more prepared for, and resilient to, such events. Parliaments cannot be relegated to second place as governments keep creating and changing emergency measures in such a repeated and unpredictable manner. Courts cannot suspend basic legal protections on the basis of contestable government-led evidence about the nature of such events. Courts and tribunals cannot have cases subject to long delays and postponements, and then suffer enormous backlogs, because they have been largely shut down. The same applies to all kinds of other decision makers, from immigration officials to urban planning committees. Entire regulatory regimes, like the Australian immigration system, cannot be effectively shut down as international borders are sealed. All of these experiences and many more speak to a systemic failure of administrative law and government more broadly during the COVID-19 pandemic:

9. A Virtual Crown Court mock trial piloted by the UK charity JUSTICE in the early days of the COVID-19 pandemic.

one with enormous social, economic, and political costs and one which we (literally) cannot afford to be repeated.

Considering the likelihood of further pandemics, natural disasters, and climate-related emergencies, we cannot see the rule of law and accountability frameworks being suspended or dismantled every time we experience a mass disruptive event. In addition, the painful irony is that the courts—which are supposed to be our guarantor of fundamental rights—waved through many pandemic restrictions without subjecting them to the rigour of standard legal tests on the basis that they were 'emergency measures' or 'policy decisions'. There was unwarranted deference shown by courts towards government judgment. For example, in the English case of *R (on the application of Dolan and others) v Secretary of State for Health and Social Care* [2020] EWCA Civ 1605, the Court of Appeal rejected the irrationality ground of review against pandemic regulations by stating that the government was entitled to take into account 'public opinion' (notwithstanding the extent to which government and the media were terrifying the population with their messaging about COVID-19) and weigh it in the balance with the effect of restrictions on much more consequential factors like public health, the economy, and education. The court stated that it should be slow to interfere with ministerial judgments about medical and scientific issues made 'after taking advice from relevant experts' (notwithstanding controversies on which experts were and were not consulted), and that pandemic restrictions were 'a matter of political judgment for the Government, which is accountable to Parliament, and is not suited to determination by the courts'.

Similarly, in the Canadian case of *Taylor v Newfoundland and Labrador*, 2020 NLSC 125, the Supreme Court of Newfoundland and Labrador upheld a travel ban between Nova Scotia and Newfoundland despite it breaching section 6 of the Canadian Charter of Rights and Freedoms on mobility rights. The court held that the travel ban was valid under section 1 of the Charter which allows for 'reasonable limits prescribed by law [to be placed on other Charter rights] as can be demonstrably justified in a free and democratic society'. The judgment stated that it was 'not an abdication of the court's responsibility' to find that the Chief Medical Officer of Health should be afforded deference because of the expertise of her office, the sudden emergency of COVID-19 as a 'novel and deadly disease', and that she faced a 'formidable challenge under difficult circumstances'. The court used this reasoning to justify a ban on a woman travelling from Nova Scotia to Newfoundland to attend the funeral of her mother.

Never in the post-Second World War period have we collectively faced such a need for judicial protection from executive overreach, and in the hour of greatest need, the courts in multiple legal systems failed to perform this basic constitutional function. Administrative law and constitutional law are checks on the power of government. When governments seek to do something extraordinary or which significantly interferes with individual rights, the law *and the courts* should be more—not less—exacting in their scrutiny for legality. Yet too many courts balked during the COVID-19 pandemic, blinded by perceived government competence and conscientiousness, scientific wisdom, and the difficulty of the task at hand. It is a matter of high concern that, post-pandemic, these lessons do not appear to have been sufficiently learned, nor has enough been done to avoid a repeat of the extreme costs of chaotic and erratic emergency management. Whereas administrative law, and the institutions that enforce it, could have used this bitter experience to be better prepared for and more resilient to the next pandemic or mass disruptive event, there is now judicial and constitutional precedent for the courts throwing their hands in the air and hoping for the best. That is a real and serious challenge for the integrity and effectiveness of administrative law.

Looking to the future in a quite different context, the 'Fourth Industrial Revolution', a phrase popularized by World Economic Forum founder Klaus Schwab, will and already is posing problems for administrative law. Digitization and digitalization raise all kinds of problems for public bodies' data security and service delivery, including the possibility for data breaches and cyber attacks by hostile actors. Automated and algorithmic decision making by public authorities can exacerbate accountability deficits as decisions are made on a 'computer says no' basis. We have already seen an example of this in our discussion of the Australian Robodebt saga in Chapter 1. Automation of decision making and resource allocation can also result in diminished understanding by public officials of how such systems work in the first place, or they might be designed in a way that does not reflect the intention behind their design, or for that matter the legal provisions that underlie those decision-making and resource allocation processes. How many lawyers understand software engineering, and how many software engineers understand the law?

The role of automated decision making in government has a longer pedigree than might be anticipated: the first statutory provision for computers to make decisions in the UK was section 2 of the Social Security Act 1998 which stated that certain decisions of the government minister 'may be made or issued not only by an officer of his acting under his authority but also by a computer for whose operation such an officer is responsible'. When AI and machine learning are introduced into the equation, computer systems may begin to mimic human decision making and resource allocation but in a way that is not fully understood, predicted, or intended. This includes the possibility for AI to be designed with built-in biases, whether intentional or unintentional, or for AI to 'learn' biases as it evolves. Will public bodies then have the resources to properly investigate what is going wrong with these systems and to fix them? Will the costs and injustices generated by them already be too great? Might AI systems evolve to a stage where they might be considered decision makers in their own right?

The problem is replicated at a more mundane level—we may increasingly find that when we try to contact a public authority about some health, education, or taxation concern we cannot speak to a human operator, but are instead presented with an automated or AI intermediary which cannot appropriately deal with our enquiry or request. There are already many examples of this in the public sector but US Citizenship and Immigration Services, an agency of the US Department of Homeland Security, is notorious in this regard—its telephone system makes it very difficult to speak with a human operator. Is that a simple matter of a government agency managing tight resources, or is it a deliberate ploy to make things difficult for ordinary people; what Professor of Law Edward Rubin called 'bureaucratic oppression'? Is it a way of weakening accountability, or could that at least be an unintended consequence? Automated and AI systems are already being used by the private sector to lighten the load of customer enquiry and complaint. That is not unproblematic but in theory a person can abandon a private company and take their custom elsewhere. The same cannot be said for public bodies. Diminishing reachability and accountability in the public sector poses real problems, including for the effectiveness of administrative law.

But it is not just about automation and AI being used as a way of relieving administrative burdens by answering helplines and resolving queries. AI is already being used in Estonia, for example, to decide certain low-level court cases. While their 'decisions' can be appealed to a human judge, we are already on the first rung of the ladder in terms of computers replacing human judges. It also raises serious questions about the private corporations that design and produce the software solutions for such AI and automation. Those corporations will in all likelihood know more about the software than their public sector clients, and be able to influence their design in ways that their public sector clients—and members of the public—do not understand. All of this has the potential to create a minefield in administrative law, where core concepts like transparency, objectivity, procedural fairness, rules against delegation, and a willingness to make exceptions come under threat. It also spells real dangers for the rule of law and broader political accountability.

All of these challenges and more besides line up to present a series of trials for the future of administrative law. The world is experiencing a turbulent and disorientating period. Economies, public health systems, and educational attainment are still reeling from a botched handling of the COVID-19 pandemic. Russia's invasion of Ukraine brought serious risks for regional and global peace but also economic and political stability; escalating conflicts in the Middle East and rising tensions in East Asia pose further such risks. Inflation and the cost-of-living crisis have been accelerating, pushed on by these factors plus general economic mismanagement. Many countries are continuing down a track of unsustainable demographics and economic decline. Information, misinformation, and disinformation have become a tangled web with as yet untold implications for social and political stability. Advances in AI have raised questions about its impact on the economy, livelihoods, and even human existence itself, and whether and how these risks are manageable. The world continues to battle natural disasters and the multifaceted effects of climate change, and health authorities tell us that the next pandemic is just around the corner. Against this backdrop, it is not surprising that the World Economic Forum's 'Global Risks Report 2025' shows a pessimistic global outlook with increasing concern about the risks of global catastrophes.

In this maelstrom of risk and uncertainty, what is the role and future of administrative law? One certainty is that administrative law, as an established feature of all countries—from liberal democracies to totalitarian states—will remain. For so long as there continue to be public health, education, welfare, immigration, taxation, urban planning, and environmental control systems to administer, there will continue to be rules about their administration. Administrative law will only cease to be of relevance in some form of societal collapse. But can it continue in its current form to perform its core role effectively in holding government accountable? Does it need to change, and if so, how? Or are the changes required elsewhere, in the broader realm of politics, the economy, and social policy, for administrative law to retain its potential?

Whatever the future holds, it is hoped that this short book raises the profile and understanding of administrative law among specialists and members of the public alike. Administrative law has a major contribution to make to effective government, democracy, and the rule of law. But that contribution can only be maximized with sufficient knowledge of the principles, rules, and institutions of administrative law among all stakeholders—legislators, officials in public authorities, commentators including academics and media, and individuals who are subject to public authority. Whether one is a taxpayer, business owner, benefits claimant, university student, public health patient, prisoner, or asylum claimant, administrative law affects every one of us in ways we cannot afford to ignore.

References

Chapter 1: What is administrative law?

Associated Provincial Picture Houses Ltd v Wednesbury Corporation [1948] 1 KB 223 (England & Wales) (UK)

Commonwealth Ombudsman, 'Centrelink's automated debt raising and recovery system: A report about the Department of Human Services' Online Compliance Intervention System for Debt Raising and Recovery' (Report 02/2017) (April 2017) https://www.ombudsman.gov.au/__data/assets/pdf_file/0022/43528/Report-Centrelinks-automated-debt-raising-and-recovery-system-April-2017.pdf (Australia)

Cooper v Wandsworth Board of Works (1863) 143 ER 414 (England & Wales) (UK)

Padfield v Minister for Agriculture, Fisheries and Food [1968] AC 997 (HL) (England & Wales) (UK)

Prygodicz v Commonwealth of Australia (No 2) [2021] FCA 634 (Australia)

R v Cambridge Health Authority, ex parte B [1995] EWCA Civ 43 (England & Wales) (UK)

R v Panel on Take-overs and Mergers, ex parte Datafin [1987] QB 815 (England & Wales) (UK)

Ridge v Baldwin [1964] AC 40 (England & Wales) (UK)

The Senate, 'Design, scope, cost-benefit analysis, contracts awarded and implementation associated with the Better Management of the Social Welfare System initiative' (June 2017) https://www.aph.gov.au/Parliamentary_Business/Committees/Senate/Community_Affairs/SocialWelfareSystem/~/media/Committees/clac_ctte/SocialWelfareSystem/report.pdf (Australia)

The Senate, 'Accountability and justice: Why we need a Royal Commission into Robodebt' (May 2022) https://parlinfo.aph.gov.au/parlInfo/download/committees/reportsen/024846/toc_pdf/AccountabilityandjusticeWhyweneedaRoyalCommissioninto Robodebt pdf;fileType=application%2Fpdf (Australia)

Chapter 2: Internal review

Administrative Procedure Act of 1946 (US)
Administrative Review Council, 'Internal Review of Agency Decision Making' (Report No. 44) (November 2000) (Australia)
Michael Asimow, 'Five models of administrative adjudication' *American Journal of Comparative Law* 63(1) (2015): 3
Constitution of the United States (US)
Freedom of Information Act 1982 (Cth) (Australia)
Freedom of Information Act 2000 (UK)
Housing Act 1996 (UK)
Immigration Rules (UK)
Loper Bright Enterprises v Raimondo, 603 US 369 (US)
Securities and Exchange Commission v Jarkesy, No. 22-859 (US)
Welfare Reform Act 2012 (UK)

Chapter 3: Administrative tribunals

Committee on Administrative Tribunals and Enquiries, 'Report of the Committee on Administrative Tribunals and Enquiries' (Cmnd Paper 218) (1957) ('Franks Report') (UK)
Commonwealth of Australia Constitution (Australia)
Carol Harlow, 'Tribunals and adversarial process: Messages from history' in Stephen Thomson, Matthew Groves, and Greg Weeks (eds), *Administrative Tribunals in the Common Law World* (Hart Publishing, 2024)
Sir Andrew Leggatt, *Tribunals for Users: One System, One Service* ('Leggatt Report') (2001)
R v Kirby, ex parte Boilermakers' Society of Australia [1956] HCA 10 (Australia)
Robert Thomas, 'UK tribunals: Structure, history and constitutional status and practice' in Stephen Thomson, Matthew Groves, and Greg Weeks (eds), *Administrative Tribunals in the Common Law World* (Hart Publishing, 2024)

Stephen Thomson, Matthew Groves, and Greg Weeks (eds), *Administrative Tribunals in the Common Law World* (Hart Publishing, 2024)

Tribunals, Courts and Enforcement Act 2007 (UK)

Chapter 4: Judicial review

Aboriginal and Torres Strait Islander Heritage Protection Act 1984 (Australia)

Administrative Decisions (Judicial Review) Act 1977 (Cth) (Australia)

Administrative Procedure Act of 1946 (US)

Administrative Process Act (Virginia) (US)

Administrative Review Tribunal Act 2024 (Cth) (Australia)

Anisminic v Foreign Compensation Commission [1969] 2 AC 147 (England & Wales) (UK)

Associated Provincial Picture Houses Ltd v Wednesbury Corporation [1948] 1 KB 223 (England & Wales) (UK)

Bagg's Case (1615) 11 Co Rep 93 (England)

Basic Law of the Hong Kong Special Administrative Region of the People's Republic of China (Hong Kong) (People's Republic of China)

Board of Education v Rice [1911] AC 179 (England & Wales) (UK)

Brant Dairy Co Ltd v Milk Commission of Ontario [1973] SCR 131 (Ontario) (Canada)

Canadian Charter of Rights and Freedoms (Canada)

Peter Cane, 'Do banks dare to lend to local authorities?' *Law Quarterly Review* 110 (1994): 514

Carltona Ltd v Commissioner of Works [1943] 2 All ER 560 (England & Wales) (UK)

Citizens to Preserve Overton Park v Volpe 401 US 402 (1971) (US)

Commonwealth of Australia Constitution (Australia)

Constitution Act 1867 (Canada)

Constitution of India (India)

Constitution of the United States (US)

Council of Civil Service Unions v Minister for the Civil Service [1985] AC 374 (England & Wales) (UK)

Crédit Suisse v Allerdale Borough Council [1997] QB 306 (England & Wales) (UK)

Crevier v Attorney General (Québec) [1981] 2 SCR 220 (Canada)

Detention of Terrorists (Northern Ireland) Order 1972 (UK)

Engel v Vitale 370 US 421(1962) (US)

Foreign Compensation Act 1950 (UK)

Gurung Bhakta Bahadur v Director of Immigration [2001] 3 HKLRD 225 (Hong Kong) (People's Republic of China)

Housing Act 2004 (UK)

Human Rights Act 1998 (UK)

Immigration and Refugee Protection Act 2001 (Canada)

Innes v Wylie (1844) 1 Car & Kir 257 (England & Wales) (UK)

Interpretation and General Clauses Ordinance (Cap. 1) (Hong Kong) (People's Republic of China)

Judiciary Act 1903 (Cth) (Australia)

Keyu v Secretary of State for Foreign and Commonwealth Affairs [2015] UKSC 69 (England & Wales) (UK)

Local Government (Contracts) Act 1997 (UK)

Marbury v Madison 5 US (1 Cranch) 137 (1803) (US)

Meng Ching Hai v Attorney-General [1991] 1 HKLR 535 (Hong Kong) (People's Republic of China)

Migration Act 1958 (Cth) (Australia)

Motor Vehicle Manufacturers Association v State Farm Mutual Automobile Insurance Co 463 US 29 (1983) (US)

Padfield v Minister for Agriculture, Fisheries and Food [1968] AC 997 (HL) (England & Wales) (UK)

Plaintiff S157/2002 v Commonwealth (2003) 211 CLR 476 (Australia)

Planning Act 2008 (UK)

R v Adams [2020] UKSC 19 (Northern Ireland) (UK)

R v Barnsley Metropolitan Borough Council, ex parte Hook [1976] 1 WLR 1052 (England & Wales) (UK)

R v Bow Street Stipendiary Magistrate, ex parte Pinochet (No 2) [2000] 1 AC 119 (England & Wales) (UK)

R v Governor of Brixton Prison, ex parte Soblen (No 2) [1963] 2 QB 243 (England & Wales) (UK)

R v North and East Devon Health Authority, ex parte Coughlan [2001] QB 213 (England & Wales) (UK)

R v Panel on Take-overs and Mergers, ex parte Datafin [1987] QB 815 (England & Wales) (UK)

R v Secretary of State for the Home Department, ex parte Venables [1998] AC 407 (England & Wales) (UK)

R x Sussex Justices, ex parte McCarthy [1924] 1 KB 256 (England & Wales) (UK)

R v Warwickshire County Council, ex parte Collymore [1995] ELR 217 (England & Wales) (UK)

R (on the application of Privacy International) v Investigatory Powers Tribunal [2019] UKSC 22 (England & Wales) (UK)
Re Brook (1864) 143 ER 1184 (England & Wales) (UK)
Re Lee Ching Ming [1990] HKCFI 224 (Hong Kong) (People's Republic of China)
Regulation of Investigatory Powers Act 2000 (UK)
Ridge v Baldwin [1964] AC 40 (England & Wales) (UK)
Sahni Silk Mills (P) Ltd v ESI Corp (1994) 5 SCC 346 (India)
Salameda v Immigration and Naturalization Service 70 F.3d 447 (7th Cir. 1995) (US)
Schlieske v Minister for Immigration and Ethnic Affairs (1988) 84 ALR 719 (Australia)
Secretary for Justice v Li Chau Wing [2004] HKCFI 1048 (Hong Kong) (People's Republic of China)
Social Welfare Consolidation Act 2005 (Ireland)
State Administrative Procedure Act (New York) (US)
Tickner v Chapman (1995) 57 FCR 451 (Australia)
Zestra Asia Ltd v Commissioner for Transport [2007] 4 HKLRD 722 (Hong Kong) (People's Republic of China)

Chapter 5: From ombudsmen to public inquiries: Other administrative law controls

Access to Information Act 1985 (Canada)
Basic Law of the Hong Kong Special Administrative Region of the People's Republic of China (Hong Kong) (People's Republic of China)
Basic Law of the Macau Special Administrative Region of the People's Republic of China (Macau) (People's Republic of China)
Tony Blair, *A Journey* (Random House, 2010)
Civil Service Code (UK)
Constitution of India (India)
Constitution of the Republic of China (Taiwan)
Constitution of the Republic of Ghana (Ghana)
Convention on Combating Bribery of Foreign Public Officials in International Business Transactions (OECD Anti-Bribery Convention)
Equality Act 2006 (UK)
Equality Act 2010 (UK)
Espionage Act of 1917 (US)
Foreign Corrupt Practices Act of 1977 (US)
Freedom of Information Act 1982 (Australia)

Freedom of Information Act 2000 (UK)
Freedom of Information Act 1967 (US)
House of Commons Canada, 'Do service well: The Standing Committee on Public Accounts of the Forty-Second Parliament' (2019) https://www.ourcommons.ca/Content/Committee/421/PACP/Reports/RP10581634/pacprp68/pacprp68-e.pdf (Canada)
Infected Blood Inquiry, *The Report* (20 May 2024) (7 Volumes) HC569 (UK)
International Monetary Fund, 'Fiscal Council Dataset' (2021) https://www.imf.org/en/Data/Fiscal/fiscal-council-dataset
INTOSAI Auditing Standards
Official Information Act 1982 (New Zealand)
R (on the application of Evans) v Attorney General [2015] UKSC 21 (England & Wales) (UK)
Transparency International, *Corruption Perceptions Index* https://www.transparency.org/en/cpi/
Venice Commission, *Principles on the Protection and Promotion of the Ombudsman Institution* (March 2019) https://www.venice.coe.int/webforms/documents/default.aspx?pdffile=CDL-AD(2019)005-e
Whistleblower Protection Act of 1989 (US)

Chapter 6: The future of administrative law

Canadian Charter of Rights and Freedoms (Canada)
House of Commons, Committee of Public Accounts, 'HMRC performance in 2022–23' HC 76 (28 February 2024) https://committees.parliament.uk/publications/43549/documents/216398/default/ (UK)
R (on the application of Dolan and others) v Secretary of State for Health and Social Care [2020] EWCA Civ 1605 (England & Wales) (UK)
Edward L. Rubin, 'Bureaucratic oppression: Its causes and cures' *Washington University Law Review* 90(2) (2012): 291
Social Security Act 1998 (UK)
Taylor v Newfoundland and Labrador [2020] NLSC 125 (Newfoundland and Labrador) (Canada)
World Economic Forum, 'The global risks report 2025' (20th edition) (2025) https://reports.weforum.org/docs/WEF_Global_Risks_Report_2025.pdf

Further reading

General

Peter Cane, Herwig C.H. Hofmann, Eric C. Ip, and Peter L. Lindseth (eds), *The Oxford Handbook of Comparative Administrative Law* (Oxford University Press, 2020)

Andrew Edgar, *Regulation-Making in the United Kingdom and Australia: Democratic Legitimacy, Safeguards and Executive Aggrandisement* (Hart Publishing, 2024)

Matthew Groves and Anita Stuhmcke (eds), *The Ombudsman in the Modern State* (Hart Publishing, 2022)

Ivan Hare, Catherine Donnelly, and Joanna Bell (eds), *De Smith's Judicial Review* (9th edition) (Sweet & Maxwell, 2023)

Robert Hazell and Timothy Foot, *Executive Power: The Prerogative, Past, Present and Future* (Hart Publishing, 2024)

Marc Hertogh and Richard Kirkham (eds), *Research Handbook on the Ombudsman* (Edward Elgar, 2018)

Marc Hertogh, Richard Kirkham, Robert Thomas, and Joe Tomlinson (eds), *The Oxford Handbook of Administrative Justice* (Oxford University Press, 2022)

Swati Jhaveri and Michael Ramsden (eds), *Judicial Review of Administrative Action Across the Common Law World* (Cambridge University Press, 2021)

Jeff King and Octávio L.M Ferraz (eds), *The Oxford Compendium of National Legal Responses to COVID-19* (Oxford University Press, 2021)

Isabelle Mitchell, Peter Watkin Jones, Sarah Jones, and Emma Ireton, *The Practical Guide to Public Inquiries* (Hart Publishing, 2023)

Regine Paul, Emma Carmel, and Jennifer Cobbe (eds), *Handbook on Public Policy and Artificial Intelligence* (Edward Elgar, 2024)

Susan Rose-Ackerman, Peter L. Lindseth, and Blake Emerson (eds), *Comparative Administrative Law* (2nd edition) (Edward Elgar, 2019)

Stephen Thomson, Matthew Groves, and Greg Weeks (eds), *Administrative Tribunals in the Common Law World* (Hart Publishing, 2024)

Jason N.E. Varuhas, *Damages and Human Rights* (Hart Publishing, 2016)

Australia

Mark Aronson, Matthew Groves, and Greg Weeks, *Judicial Review of Administrative Action and Government Liability* (7th edition) (Thomson Reuters Australia, 2021)

Robin Creyke, Matthew Groves, John McMillan, and Mark Smyth, *Control of Government Action: Text, Cases and Commentary* (LexisNexis, 2021)

Canada

Sara Blake, *Administrative Law in Canada* (7th edition) (LexisNexis Canada, 2022)

Paul Daly, *Administrative Law in Context* (4th edition) (Emond Publishing, 2021)

Hong Kong

Stephen Thomson, *Administrative Law in Hong Kong* (Cambridge University Press, 2018)

India

M.P. Jain and S.N. Jain, *Principles of Administrative Law* (9th edition) (LexisNexis, 2021)

Ireland

Gerard Hogan, David Gwynn Morgan, and Paul Daly, *Administrative Law in Ireland* (5th edition) (Roundhall, 2019)

New Zealand

Philip A. Joseph, *Joseph on Constitutional and Administrative Law* (5th edition) (Thomson Reuters, 2021)

Singapore

Kevin Y.L. Tan and Thio Li-ann, *Constitutional and Administrative Law in Singapore: Cases, Materials and Commentary* (4th edition) (Academy Publishing, 2021)

South Africa

Cora Hoexter and Glenn Penfold, *Administrative Law in South Africa* (3rd edition) (Juta, 2021)

United Kingdom: England and Wales

Paul Craig, *Administrative Law* (9th edition) (Sweet & Maxwell, 2021)
C.F. Forsyth and I.J. Ghosh, *Wade & Forsyth's Administrative Law* (12th edition) (Oxford University Press, 2022)
Government Legal Department, *The Judge Over Your Shoulder* (6th edition) (2022) https://assets.publishing.service.gov.uk/media/632c177f8fa8f53caf9d68a9/The_Judge_Over_Your_Shoulder_JOYS_6th_edition_2022.pdf
Ivan Hare, Catherine Donnelly, and Joanna Bell (eds), *De Smith's Judicial Review* (9th edition) (Sweet & Maxwell, 2023)
Carol Harlow and Richard Rawlings, *Law and Administration* (4th edition) (Cambridge University Press, 2021)

United Kingdom: Northern Ireland

Gordon Anthony, *Judicial Review in Northern Ireland* (3rd edition) (Hart Publishing, 2024)

United Kingdom: Scotland

Stephen Thomson and Denis Edwards (eds), 'Administrative law (2nd reissue)' in *The Laws of Scotland: The Stair Memorial Encyclopaedia* (Vol. 1) (LexisNexis, 2023)

United States

Michael Asimow and Ronald M. Levin, *State and Federal Administrative Law* (5th edition) (West Academic Publishing, 2020)

Kristin E. Hickman and Richard J. Pierce, Jr., *Administrative Law Treatise* (7th edition) (Wolters Kluwer, 2024)

Peter L. Strauss, *Administrative Justice in the United States* (3rd edition) (Carolina Academic Press, 2016)

Kathryn A. Watts, Michael Herz, and Richard W. Murphy (eds), *A Guide to Judicial and Political Review of Federal Agencies* (2nd edition) (American Bar Association, 2015)

Index

For the benefit of digital users, indexed terms that span two pages (e.g., 52–53) may, on occasion, appear on only one of those pages.

A

Aboriginal and Torres Strait Islander Heritage Protection Act 1984 (Australia) 49–50
abuse of discretion 62
abuse of power 47–8
Access to Information Act 1985 (Canada) 96–7
access to justice 16–18, 23, 30, 70, 103–4
accountability 10, 12–13, 16–17, 23, 28–9, 33, 62, 70, 73–4, 78–9, 82–3, 89–90, 94–7, 101–11
accounts committees, parliamentary, see *parliamentary accounts committees*
Adams, Gerry 51–2
adjudication 21
Administrative Appeals Board (Hong Kong) 27
Administrative Decisions (Judicial Review) Act 1977 (Australia) 41, 43–4, 56
administrative law judges 21–3
Administrative Procedure Act (New York) 68
Administrative Procedure Act of 1946 (USA) 21–3, 38, 43–4, 56–7, 62, 68
Administrative Process Act (Virginia) 68
Administrative Review Council (Australia) 16–17
Administrative Review Tribunal (Australia) 25–8, 31–2, 66
Administrative Review Tribunal Act 2024 (Australia) 66
administrative tribunals 4–6, 19–32, 95–6
agencies (USA) 21–2, 31–2, 62, 68, 74–5
AI, *see* artificial intelligence
Anisminic v Foreign Compensation Commission [1969] 2 AC 147 55
Anti-Bribery Convention 86
anti-corruption, see *corruption*
appeal (right of) 19–20, 22–5, 28, 36–7, 65–6

Army–McCarthy hearings 76
artificial intelligence 13–14, 101, 104, 108–11
Associated Provincial Picture Houses Ltd v Wednesbury Corporation [1948] 1 KB 223 7–8, 48–9, 58
audit, *see* financial integrity and public audit bodies
Australia 8–9, 25–9, 34–5, 38–41, 43–4, 49–50, 54, 56–8, 62, 64, 66, 72–3, 75–6, 79, 87–8, 90–6, 98–9, 108
Australian Constitution 27, 29–31, 41, 43, 56–7, 64
Australian Energy Regulator 95
Australian Human Rights Commission 83–4
Australian National Audit Office 92–3
Australian National Preventive Health Agency 96
automation 108–11

B

Bagg's Case (1615) 11 Co Rep 93 65
Bankman-Fried, Sam 91–2
Basic Law of the Hong Kong Special Administrative Region 43, 52, 88–9
Basic Law of the Macau Special Administrative Region 88–9
bias 16–17, 21–2, 66–8
Blair, Tony 98–9
Bloody Sunday Inquiry 82–3, 104
Board of Education v Rice [1911] AC 179 65–6
Brant Dairy Co Ltd v Milk Commission of Ontario [1973] SCR 131 52
breach of statutory procedure 46–7
Browne-Wilkinson, Lord 52–3

C

Canada 27, 34–5, 38, 52, 56–8, 64, 72–6, 90–4, 96–7, 99
Canadian Charter of Rights and Freedoms 43, 107
Canadian Human Rights Commission 83–4
Carltona Ltd v Commissioner of Works [1943] 2 All ER 560 50–2
Carltona principle 50–2
Central Bureau of Investigation (India) 87–8
Central Vigilance Commission (India) 87–8
Charles, Prince 100
Chevron deference 22
children 1–3, 52–3, 79, 83–4
China 48, 88–9
Citizens to Preserve Overton Park v Volpe 401 US 402 (1971) 62
civil law systems 11, 73, 88–9, 93–4
Civil Service Code (UK) 91
Civil Service Commission (UK) 91
Civilian Review and Complaints Commission for the Royal Canadian Mounted Police 91
Clinton, Hillary 7, 77–8
Coleman, Norm 7
Commission Against Corruption (Macau) 88–9
Committee of Public Accounts (Ireland) 94
Commonwealth Ombudsman (Australia) 9
complaints procedures (parliamentary) 73–5
Congress (US) 76
Congressional Budget Office 93–4
congressional committees 7, 75–9

considerations, irrelevant or impermissible 48–50
consistency 17–18
Constitution (Australia) 27, 29–31, 41, 43, 56–7, 64
Constitution (Ghana) 92–3
Constitution (India) 56–7
Constitution (Taiwan) 73
Constitution (US) 22, 65–6, 68
Constitution Act 1867 (Canada) 56–7
constitutional law 3, 11–12, 29, 33–4, 43, 59–60, 64–6, 105–8
Convention on Combating Bribery of Foreign Public Officials in International Business Transactions (Anti-Bribery Convention) 86
Cooper v Wandsworth Board of Works (1863) 143 ER 414 6
corruption 85–9, 91–2
Corruption and Crime Commission (Western Australia) 88–9
Council of Civil Service Unions v Minister for the Civil Service [1985] AC 374 44, 59–60, 63
COVID-19 7, 106–8, 110–11
COVID-19 Inquiry (UK) 7
Crédit Suisse v Allerdale Borough Council [1997] QB 306 42
Crevier v Attorney General (Québec) [1981] 2 SCR 220 56–7

D

Datafin 7–8
deference 22
delegation, unlawful 50–2
Department for Work and Pensions (UK) 19–20
Department of Health (Australia) 96
Department of Justice (US) 91–2
deportation 47–8
Detention of Terrorists (Northern Ireland) Order 1972 (UK) 51–2
digitalization 108–10
Diplock, Lord 44–5, 59–60, 63
disclosure, duty of 65–6
discretion 45–6, 48–54, 56–7, 61–2
discrimination 11–12, 82–5
disqualification (bias) 67–8
due process 68

E

education 3, 6–7, 39, 43, 53, 74, 84–5, 95, 106–7, 109
elections 91–2
Election Commission of India 91–2
Electoral Commission (Ireland) 91–2
Electoral Commission (UK) 91–2
Engel v Vitale 370 US 421 (1962) 43
environment 13–14, 37–8
Environmental Protection Agency (Ireland) 95
Equality Act 2006 (UK) 83
Equality Act 2010 (UK) 83
Equality and Human Rights Commission 83–4
errors in decision-making 16–17, 54–7
Espionage Act of 1917 (US) 89–90
ethics 10, 17–18, 23
European Convention on Human Rights 59–60, 63–4
European Union law 63–4
excess of statutory power 46–7
executive agencies (USA) 21–2, 31–2, 62, 68, 74–5
extradition 47–8

F

fairness, *see* procedural fairness
Federal Bureau of Investigation 86–7
Federal Election Commission (US) 91–2
Federal Register (US) 21
Felt, W. Mark 7, 89–90
fettering of discretion 52–3
finance 40–2, 69, 91–5, 101, 110–11
Finance and Expenditure Committee (New Zealand) 94
financial integrity and public audit bodies 91–5
Financial Markets Authority (New Zealand) 95
Finland 73
First-tier Tribunal (UK) 19–20, 27–8
fiscal councils 93–4
FOI, *see* freedom of information
Foreign Compensation Act 1950 (UK) 55
Foreign Corrupt Practices Act of 1977 (US) 86–7
Fourth Industrial Revolution 108
freedom of information 3–5, 15, 20–1, 85–6, 96–100
Freedom of Information Act 1982 (Australia) 20–1, 96–7
Freedom of Information Act 2000 (UK) 96–100
Freedom of Information Act of 1967 (US) 96–7

G

Galloway, George 7, 77–8
Ghana 92–3
Global Alliance of National Human Rights Institutions 85
Government Accountability Office (US) 92–3
Greene, Lord 48–9, 58
Grenfell Tower Inquiry 7, 79
Gurung Bhakta Bahadur v Director of Immigration [2001] 3 HKLRD 225 55–6

H

Harding, Warren G 86–7
health 1–2, 6–8, 13–14, 38–40, 58, 72–4, 80–2, 84–5, 96, 101–3
hearings 21–2, 57–8, 65–6, 68
Hewart, Lord 66–7
His Majesty's Revenue and Customs, *see* HMRC
Historical Institutional Abuse Inquiry 79
HMRC 19–20, 102–3
Hoffmann, Lord 67
Home Office (UK) 18, 96
Hong Kong 24–9, 31–2, 34–5, 38, 52, 62, 64, 66–8, 72–3, 75, 88–9, 91
housing 3, 6–7, 19, 28–9
Housing Act 1996 (UK) 19
Housing Act 2004 (UK) 43–4
human rights 4–5, 11–12, 39–40, 59–60, 62, 64, 82–5
Human Rights Act 1998 (UK) 59–60
human rights monitors 82–5

I

immigration 3–4, 6–7, 11–12, 18–19, 27–9, 39–40, 43–4, 47–8, 74–5, 105–6
Immigration and Refugee Protection Act 2001 (Canada) 43–4
Immigration Rules (UK) 18
impartiality 10, 16–17, 21–2, 31–2, 66–8
improper motives 47–8
improper purposes 47–9

India 27, 31–2, 38, 52, 56–8, 64, 84, 87–8, 91–3
Indian Constitution 56–7, 91–2
Independent Commission Against Corruption (Hong Kong) 88–9
Independent Office for Police Conduct (UK) 91
Independent Parliamentary Standards Authority 85–6
Independent Police Complaints Council (Hong Kong) 91
Infected Blood Inquiry 79–82
information, freedom of, *see* freedom of information
Information Commissioner (Ireland) 99
Information Commissioner's Office (UK) 99
inherent jurisdiction 28, 56–7
Innes v Wylie (1844) 1 Car & Kir 257 65–6
inquiries, *see* public inquiries
integrity, *see* financial integrity and public audit bodies, public service integrity bodies
Internal Revenue Service—Criminal Investigation 86–7
internal review 4–6, 15–23
International Ombudsman Institute 73–4, 88–9
International Organization of Supreme Audit Institutions (INTOSAI) 93–5
interpretation, *see* statutory interpretation
Interpretation and General Clauses Ordinance (Hong Kong) 55–6
investigations 71–2
Iraq Inquiry 7, 79
Ireland 38, 54, 58, 64, 75–6, 91–5, 99
irrationality 58–62, 64
Israel 24, 27–8

J

Jarkesy 22
Joint Committee of Public Accounts and Audit (Australia) 94
judges 21–2, 25–6, 30–1, 88, 65–8, 85, 91–2, 110
judicial review 6, 16–17, 19, 22–3, 25–6, 28, 33–68, 70–1
 grounds of 42–68
 procedure 36–42
Judiciary Act 1903 (Australia) 41

K

Keyu v Secretary of State for Foreign and Commonwealth Affairs [2015] UKSC 69 64

L

Legislative Council Redress System (Hong Kong) 75
legitimate expectations 57–8
licensing 2–3, 6–8, 27–9, 38, 43–6, 48, 57–8, 60–1, 63, 81, 95–6
Local Government (Contracts) Act 1997 (UK) 42
Lokayukta 87–8
Loper Bright Enterprises v Raimondo, 603 US 369 22

M

Macau 88–9
McBride, David 90–1
McCarthy, Joseph 76
Manchester Arena Inquiry 7, 79
Manning, Chelsea 7, 89–90
Marbury v Madison 5 US (1 Cranch) 137 (1803) 43
mediation 30, 71–2
Meng Ching Hai v Attorney-General [1991] 1 HKLR 535 48

Merit Systems Protection Board 90
merits (review) 25–6, 28–30, 35–6, 58, 61, 63–4
Migration Act 1958 (Australia) 43–4
motives 47–9
Motor Vehicle Manufacturers Association v State Farm Mutual Automobile Insurance Co 463 US 29 (1983) 62

N

National Anti-Corruption Commission (Australia) 87–8
National Audit Office (UK) 92–4
National Commission for Backward Classes 84
National Commission for Protection of Child Rights 84
National Commission for Scheduled Castes 84
National Crime Agency (UK) 87–8
National Human Rights Commission of India 84
Netherlands 73, 93–4
Netherlands Bureau for Economic Policy Analysis 93–4
New Zealand 27–8, 38, 54, 58, 64, 94–7, 99
NHS England 95
Nixon, Richard 76–7, 86–7, 89–90
Northern Ireland 51–2, 92–3

O

Office for Budget Responsibility (UK) 93–4
Office of Special Counsel 90
Office of the Australian Information Commissioner 99
Office of the Information Commissioner (Canada) 99
Office of the Inspector General 86–7
Office of the Ombudsman (Hong Kong) 75, 88–9
Office of the Public Sector Integrity Commissioner of Canada 90
Official Information Act 1982 (New Zealand) 96–7
ombudsman 4–6, 9, 69–75, 84, 87–9, 99
ouster clauses 55–7
outsourcing 19, 39–40, 42, 101–2

P

Padfield v Minister for Agriculture, Fisheries and Food [1968] AC 997 (HL) 7–8, 47
parliamentary accounts committees 94–5
Parliamentary and Health Service Ombudsman 72, 74
Parliamentary Budget Office (Australia) 93–4
Parliamentary Budget Office (Canada) 93–4
parliamentary committees 75–9
parliamentary complaints procedures 73–5
Permanent Subcommittee on Investigations (US Senate) 7, 76–8
Plaintiff S157/2002 v Commonwealth (2003) 211 CLR 476 56–7
planning 3, 6–7, 30–1, 38, 43–4, 49, 57–8, 66, 105–6
Planning Act 2008 (UK) 49
police 6–7, 38, 52, 60–1, 65–6, 87–8, 91, 101
policies 30, 52–3, 92, 96–7
Post Office Horizon IT Inquiry 7, 79–80

prisons 39–40, 48, 52–3
private law 3–4, 34–5, 38–42, 101–2
privative clauses, *see* ouster clauses
procedural fairness 9–10, 16–17, 58, 64–8
procedure 29–30, 36–42, 46–7, 57–8, 64, 71, 78–9, 82–4
proportionality 62–4
Prygodicz v Commonwealth of Australia (No 2) [2021] FCA 634 9
Public Accounts Committee (UK) 86, 94, 102–3
public health 1–2, 7–8, 11–12, 106–7
public inquiries 7, 78–83
Public Integrity Section (US) 91–2
public law 3–4, 38–42
public resources 1–2, 13–14, 16–17, 37, 42, 53, 57–8, 71–2, 97–8, 101–4, 110–11
Public Service Commission of Canada 90
public service integrity bodies 88–92
public trust 13–14, 104–5, 110–11
public/private divide 38–42, 101–2

R

R v Adams [2020] UKSC 19 51–2
R v Barnsley Metropolitan Borough Council, ex parte Hook [1976] 1 WLR 1052 63
R v Bow Street Stipendiary Magistrate, ex parte Pinochet (No 2) [2000] 1 AC 119 67
R v Cambridge Health Authority, ex parte B [1995] EWCA Civ 43 1–3
R v Governor of Brixton Prison, ex parte Soblen (No 2) [1963] 2 QB 243 48
R v Kirby, ex parte Boilermakers' Society of Australia [1956] HCA 10 29
R v North and East Devon Health Authority, ex parte Coughlan [2001] QB 213 58
R v Panel on Take-overs and Mergers, ex parte Datafin [1987] QB 815 7–8, 40–1
R v Secretary of State for the Home Department, ex parte Venables [1998] AC 407 52–3
R v Sussex Justices, ex parte McCarthy [1924] 1 KB 256 66–7
R v Warwickshire County Council, ex parte Collymore [1995] ELR 217 53
R (on the application of Dolan and others) v Secretary of State for Health and Social Care [2020] EWCA Civ 1605 106–7
R (on the application of Evans) v Attorney General [2015] UKSC 21 100
R (on the application of Privacy International) v Investigatory Powers Tribunal [2019] UKSC 22 55
rationality, *see* irrationality
Re Brook (1864) 143 ER 1184 65–6
Re Lee Ching Ming [1990] HKCFI 224 48
reasons for decisions 66
Regulations of Investigatory Powers Act 2000 (UK) 55
regulators 94–6, 103–4
remedies (judicial) 34–6
reports 71–2, 80–2
resources, public 1–2, 13–14, 16–17, 37, 42, 53, 57–8, 71–2, 97–8, 101–4, 110–11
Ridge v Baldwin [1964] AC 40 65–6

Robodebt 8–9, 108
Royal Commission into Institutional Responses to Child Sexual Abuse 79
Royal Commission into Misconduct in the Banking, Superannuation and Financial Services Industry 79
Royal Commission into National Natural Disaster Arrangements 79
Royal Commission into the Robodebt Scheme 9, 79
Royal Commission into Violence, Abuse, Neglect and Exploitation of People with Disability 79
Royal Commissions (Australia) 79
rule of law 33, 37–8, 56, 104–7, 110–11

S

Sahni Silk Mills (P) Ltd v ESI Corp (1994) 5 SCC 346 52
Salameda v Immigration and Naturalization Service 70 F.3d 447 (7th Cir. 1995) 62
Schlieske v Minister for Immigration and Ethnic Affairs (1988) 84 ALR 719 47–8
Scotland 64, 92–3
Secretary for Justice v Li Chau Wing [2004] HKCFI 1048 67–8
Securities and Exchange Commission v Jarkesy, No. 22-859 22
Select Committee on Events Surrounding the 2012 Terrorist Attack in Benghazi (US Senate) 77
Select Committee on Presidential Campaign Activities (US Senate) 76–7
separation of powers 21–2, 25–7, 30–2, 35–6, 57–8, 61–4, 107–8
Serious Fraud Office 87–8
Singapore 27–8
Snowden, Edward 7, 89–90
Social Welfare Consolidation Act 2005 (Ireland) 43–4
South Africa 24, 54, 58
Special Counsel, *see* Office of Special Counsel
standing 37–8
Standing Committee on Public Accounts (Canada) 94
statutory interpretation 22, 29, 44, 46, 48–9, 51–2, 54, 56–7

T

Taiwan 73
taxation 19–20, 22–3, 28–9, 54, 97, 102–3
Taylor v Newfoundland and Labrador, 2020 NLSC 125 107
Thailand 73
Tickner v Chapman (1995) 57 FCR 451 49–50
tribunals 4–6, 19–32, 95–6
Tribunals, Courts and Enforcement Act 2007 (UK) 26–7
Trump, Donald 12–13, 77

U

UK Border Agency 96
UK COVID-19 Inquiry 7, 79

ultra vires, *see* excess of statutory power
UN Human Rights Council 85
United States of America 36–7, 43–4, 56–7, 62, 65–6, 68, 72–5, 92–3, 96–8
unreasonableness 53–62
Upper Tribunal (UK) 27–8, 100
US Commission on Civil Rights 84
US Constitution 22, 43, 65–6, 68

V

values of administrative law 10, 64–7, 70, 82–3

W

Wales 92–3
Watergate scandal 76–7, 86–7
Welfare Reform Act 2012 (UK) 19–20
Whistleblower Protection Act of 1989 (US) 90
whistleblowing 89–91

Z

Zestra Asia Ltd v Commissioner for Transport [2007] 4 HKLRD 722 60–1

LAW
A Very Short Introduction
Raymond Wacks

Law underlies our society - it protects our rights, imposes duties on each of us, and establishes a framework for the conduct of almost every social, political, and economic activity. The punishment of crime, compensation of the injured, and the enforcement of contracts are merely some of the tasks of a modern legal system. It also strives to achieve justice, promote freedom, and protect our security. This *Very Short Introduction* provides a clear, jargon-free account of modern legal systems, explaining how the law works both in the Western tradition and around the world.

www.oup.com/vsi

EUROPEAN UNION LAW
A Very Short Introduction
Anthony Arnull

The European Union is rarely out of the news and faces difficult questions about its future. In this debate, the law always has a central role to play.

In this *Very Short Introduction* Anthony Arnull looks at the laws and legal system of the European Union, including EU courts. He discusses the range of issues that the European Union has been given the power to regulate, such as the free movement of goods and people. Arnull considers why an organisation based on international treaties has proved capable of having far-reaching influence on both its Member States and on countries that lie beyond its borders.

www.oup.com/vsi

ENVIRONMENTAL LAW
A Very Short Introduction
Elizabeth Fisher

Environmental law is the law concerned with environmental problems. It is a vast area of law that operates from the local to the global, involving a range of different legal and regulatory techniques. In theory, environmental protection is a no brainer. Few people would actively argue for pollution or environmental destruction. Ensuring a clean environment is ethically desirable, and also sensible from a purely self-interested perspective. Yet, in practice, environmental law is a messy and complex business fraught with conflict. Whilst environmental law is often characterized in overly simplistic terms, with a law being seen as be a simple solution to environmental problems, the reality is that creating and maintaining a body of laws to address and avoid problems is not easy, and involves legislators, courts, regulators, and communities.

This *Very Short Introduction* provides an overview of the main features of environmental law, and discusses how environmental law deals with multiple interests, socio-political conflicts, and the limits of knowledge about the environment. Showing how interdependent societies across the world have developed robust and legitimate bodies of law to address environmental problems, Elizabeth Fisher discusses some of the major issues and controversies involved in environmental law.

www.oup.com/vsi

PHILOSOPHY OF LAW
A Very Short Introduction
SECOND EDITION
Raymond Wacks

The concept of law lies at the heart of our social and political life. Legal philosophy, or jurisprudence, explores the notion of law and its role in society, illuminating its meaning and its relation to the universal questions of justice, rights, and morality.

In this *Very Short Introduction* Raymond Wacks analyses the nature and purpose of the legal system, and the practice by courts, lawyers, and judges. Wacks reveals the intriguing and challenging nature of legal philosophy with clarity and enthusiasm, providing an enlightening guide to the central questions of legal theory.

In this revised edition Wacks makes a number of updates including new material on legal realism, changes to the approach to the analysis of law and legal theory, and updates to historical and anthropological jurisprudence.

www.oup.com/vsi

Human Rights
A Very Short Introduction
Andrew Clapham

An appeal to human rights in the face of injustice can be a heartfelt and morally justified demand for some, while for others it remains merely an empty slogan. Taking an international perspective and focusing on highly topical issues such as torture, arbitrary detention, privacy, health and discrimination, this *Very Short Introduction* will help readers to understand for themselves the controversies and complexities behind this vitally relevant issue. Looking at the philosophical justification for rights, the historical origins of human rights and how they are formed in law, Andrew Clapham explains what our human rights actually are, what they might be, and where the human rights movement is heading.

www.oup.com/vsi

PUBLIC HEALTH
A Very Short Introduction
Virginia Berridge

Public health is a term much used in the media, by health professionals, and by activists. But what do we mean when we speak about 'public health'?

In this *Very Short Introduction* Virginia Berridge explores the areas which fall under the remit of public health, and explains how the individual histories of different countries have come to cause great differences in the perception of the role and responsibilities of public health organisations. Drawing on a wide range of international examples, Berridge demonstrates the central role of history to understanding the amorphous nature of public health today.

www.oup.com/vsi

INTERNATIONAL RELATIONS
A Very Short Introduction
Paul Wilkinson

Of undoubtable relevance today, in a post-9-11 world of growing political tension and unease, this *Very Short Introduction* covers the topics essential to an understanding of modern international relations. Paul Wilkinson explains the theories and the practice that underlies the subject, and investigates issues ranging from foreign policy, arms control, and terrorism, to the environment and world poverty. He examines the role of organizations such as the United Nations and the European Union, as well as the influence of ethnic and religious movements and terrorist groups which also play a role in shaping the way states and governments interact. This up-to-date book is required reading for those seeking a new perspective to help untangle and decipher international events.

www.oup.com/vsi